RIVERINE

A Pictorial History of the Brown Water War in Vietnam

By JIM MESKO

Illustrated by Don Greer

squadron/signal publications inc.

PBR 105, under the command of Boatswain's Mate 1st Class James Williams, fires on Viet Cong junks, sampans, and shore positions during a patrol on 31 October 1966. As a result of this action Williams was awarded the Congressional Medal of Honor.

COPYRIGHT © 1985
SQUADRON/SIGNAL PUBLICATIONS, INC.
1115 CROWLEY DRIVE, CARROLLTON, TEXAS 75011-5010

If you have any photographs of the aircraft, armor, soldiers or ships of any nation, particularly wartime snapshots, why not share them with us and help make Squadron/Signal's books all the more interesting and complete in the future. Any photograph sent to us will be copied and the original returned. The donor will be fully credited for any photos used. Please indicate if you wish us not to return the photos. Please send them to: Squadron/Signal Publications, Inc., 1115 Crowley Dr., Carrollton, TX 75011-5010.

ISBN 0-89747-163-6

Dedication:

This book is dedicated to the officers and men of the Brown Water Navy who served so valiantly for the cause of freedom. May it also serve as a memorial to those who made the ultimate sacrifice in the service of their country.

And to my father

Peter Mesko, the finest man I have ever known, whom I owe more than I can ever repay.

Credits

As is the case in any book there are a number of people whose help was indispensable. Without a doubt the key person in providing help was Bob Cressman, who provided unpublished material, photos, and other material without which this book could not have been written. He also answered numerous questions during late night telephone calls which proved extremely helpful in nailing down certain key points. Another person who provided very important information was Roy Wiggs, who provided invaluable information on VAL-4. Finally, I owe a particular debt of gratitude to my mother who proof read my rough drafts and typed the final copies, even though this took time away from her holiday preparations, and my wife who suffered through this writing with a great deal of good grace. Other people and organizations who helped out in equal fashion are listed below.

US Navy
US Coast Guard
US Army
John Maze
George Balin — Coast Guard
Dana Bell — Patrol Planes
Richard O'Mara — PCFs, Vietnamese
Howard Jacobs — General
Gerry Beneditti — RAD Units
Roy Grossnick — Patrol Planes
Bruce Simmard — Riverine Boats and PBRs
Dan Smiley — HAL-3, VAL-4
Bob Chenoweth — HAL-3
George Piter — VAL-4
Naval History Museum — French Material
Naval Aviation History and Archives Section — Patrol Planes
Peter Mersky — VAL-4
Bill Paget

Author's Note

In the fall of 1971 I received orders assigning me to a naval advisory team in the Republic of Vietnam. During this period I came into personal contact with many of the men of the Brown Water Navy who participated in the actions which are related in the following pages. In particular I met men from HAL-3, VAL-4, and SEAL detachments, as well as American trained Vietnamese naval officers and enlisted men. I was able to visit a number of bases and photograph various river craft and aircraft, some of which appear in this book. While this background helped immensely in the research and writing of this text it also made it somewhat difficult to remain objective. Throughout this book there can be ascertained a certain pride in the accomplishments which the brave men of the Brown Water Navy achieved. Their story is one which demonstrates that the American sailor in Vietnam exhibited the same raw courage which countless sailors before them exhibited in all the wars in which the US Navy has been called upon to serve. The Vietnam War is still considered by many to be a stain on American history, and the men who served in Vietnam have yet to receive the credit they so rightfully deserve. Perhaps in a small way this book will help to set a part of the record straight.

Introduction
The Brown Water War

The war in Vietnam was often a study in contrasts. No better illustration of this can be found than in the role played by the United States Navy. In the Tonkin Gulf naval aviators, flying supersonic jets off the decks of huge super carriers, participated in the aerial campaign against North Vietnam, while cruisers and the Battleship New Jersey bombarded enemy coastal areas. Further south, a vast array of small craft, few of which were ocean going, carried out a variety of tasks along the coast and up the various rivers and canals which dissected this war torn land. And while much has been written about the aerial and bombardment campaign, little has been written about these small craft in the war. Yet in terms of men, ships, action, and heroism this little known aspect of the Navy's war in Vietnam deserves equal treatment with the more glamorous big-ship operations that caught the public's attention through newspaper reports and television. The sailors who manned these small fragile boats and often fought pitched battles with the *Viet Cong* (VC) and North Vietnamese Army (NVA) at small arms range and on occasion even had to repel boarders! The kind of warfare that was waged on the inland and coastal waters of Vietnam was last practiced by the United States Navy during the Civil War, almost exactly one-hundred years earlier. As a result much of the tactics were based on the earlier experiences of the French Union Forces, or were developed through trial and error. Mistakes were made, as was to be expected, but in the end the resourceful individual sailors of these varied forces learned their lessons well and were forged into formidable fighting forces which deprived the enemy the use of these waterways.

In *RIVERINE*, I have tried to present a broad outline of the operations by the *Brown Water Navy*, as these forces came to be known, from their inception to the withdrawal of US Forces from Vietnam. The scope of this book covers the three major components of the Navy's *riverine* force and their subsidiary units. Each had its own distinct function but also worked in conjunction with the other two components when the situation dictated. Task force 115 (Market Time), had the responsibility for coastal patrol, surveillance, and interception of enemy gun runners on the high seas. Using equipment that ranged from Patrol aircraft such as the Neptune and Orion to small Swift Boats, which even included US Coast Guard cutters, Market Time carried out the usually monotonous duty of interdicting communist supplies along the coast of Vietnam. Task Force 116 (Game Warden), carried the war as far up the rivers and canals of Vietnam as their shallow draft boats would go. Using various modified landing craft, armored power boats, helicopters and even fixed wing Broncos, they eventually swept the *Viet Cong* from the Mekong Delta. The final component of the Brown Water Navy, Task Force 117 (Mobile Riverine Force), was equipped with gunboats, Armored Troop Carriers, refuelers, and a Brigade of the 9th Infantry to provide a self contained strike force that could operate through the roadless Mekong Delta in order to engage enemy forces. Collectively these riverine units made up the *Brown Water Navy*.

Today, there are many sailors who proudly wear the Vietnam Service Medal on their chest. Of these men, only a small portion served in the riverine forces. And in a sense these men are a group unto themselves. Their war was far different from that waged by the ships of the 7th Fleet in the South China Sea. Their uniforms were not whites nor even blue denims, but jungle fatigues. Their weapons were not F-4 Phantoms, 16 inch guns, or missiles, but M-16 rifles, M-79 grenade launchers, machine guns, and on occasion — knives. And rather than the traditional navy white hat, they wore a distinctive headgear, which only those who served in-country were permitted to wear. This is their story, the story of the sailors who proudly wore the Black Beret, the men of the *riverine force*.

FRENCH INDOCHINA WAR

French River Forces

In September of 1945, with the surrender of Japan, the various European countries moved to reestablish control over their colonies in the Far East. France, in particular, because of limited forces, a poor road network, difficult terrain and fierce native opposition under the leadership of Ho Chi Min, faced a monumental job in reoccupying Indochina*. Because France lacked both trained troops, and the ability to move them into the area quickly, the British and Chinese were assigned the task of accepting the surrender of Japanese troops and of governing the area until the arrival of French forces. Each moved into Indochina to accept the Japanese surrender, the Chinese marching south to the 16th parallel while the British landed in Saigon and moved north to the 16th parallel line.

Following the defeat of Germany in the spring of 1945, even before the Japanese surrender, the French had begun sending the nucleus of their reoccupation forces out from Europe. Included in these forces were certain naval units which were designated the Naval Brigade Far East. Like the majority of the other French forces, the sudden Japanese surrender came before the Brigade's ships and men had arrived, it was not until 19 October that the first elements of the Naval Brigade arrived at Saigon.

Upon its arrival, the Brigade was quickly pressed into service to help clean out pockets of *Viet Minh* resistance in Saigon following an uprising at the beginning of October. After the successful completion of this mopping up French forces spread out from Saigon to reoccupy the surrounding countryside. The Naval Brigade was assigned the job of helping retake the provincial capitals of My Tho, Vinh Long, and Can Tho. In light of future operations these early missions came off without serious problems or heavy casualties. Using a variety of captured junks, launches and miscellaneous boats, along with their own landing craft, the brigade supported an overland thrust by mechanized Army units against My Tho in late October. However, sabotaged roads and flooded rice paddies severely hampered the land drive, so the naval forces, arriving at My Tho ahead of the mechanized column, reoccupied the city before the Army arrived.

While this operation was taking place another contingent of the Naval Brigade, onboard the sloop Annamite, helped an Army column seize Vinh Long on 29 October. Fortunately these Army troops did not experience the same road conditions as the ones at My Tho had, and meeting only minimal resistance the operation went off without a hitch. The next day a small contingent from the Naval Brigade took Can Tho against spirited communist resistance. Once the city was taken the sailors began carrying out a series of raids, patrols, and ambushes to create the impression that they had sizeable forces at their disposal. The ruse worked until a second part of the brigade arrived in mid-November to reinforce them. With these additional forces, operations were expanded around the town until most of the area was secured.

These initial successes of the Naval Brigade greatly impressed the commander of the French forces, General Leclerc. In November, he ordered Captain Francois Jaubert of the Naval Brigade to create a permanent river flotilla of small craft with its own landing force. Initially called the Naval Infantry River Flotilla, this unit was assigned the task of securing the area from Saigon south to My Tho and Vinh Long. Jaubert had to literally start from scratch, but within a few weeks he had scrounged up a motley collection of captured Japanese and *Viet Minh* junks, motor launches, barges, and steamers. In December the old aircraft carrier Bearn arrived in Saigon carrying fourteen LCAs and six LCVPs, for Jaubert's flotilla. These reinforcements brought the unit up to near full strength, and, with two companies of naval infantry, Jaubert began conducting mopping up exercises in the Saigon area. In January, the flotilla supported a drive by army units to pacify the area north and east of Saigon. The largest operation of this drive was an advance up the Dong Nai river which ran northeast from Saigon toward Dalat. Unfortunately, on the last day of the operation, Captain Jaubert was killed during heavy fighting near Bien Hoa. Though his death was a severe blow to the river squadron, Jaubert left behind a foundation which would eventually span two wars and grow into a formidable force some twenty years later.

While Cochin China was being secured, other elements of the Naval Brigade, along with the 9th Colonial Infantry Division were sent from Saigon to the Tonkin region of northern Indochina aboard the Bearn. However, in late February, when the Bearn tried to enter Haiphong, the chief Vietnamese port on the Gulf of Tonkin, it was met with heavy fire from occupying Chinese troops and forced to withdraw. After negotiations, the Chinese agreed to pull their troops back and allowed the French troops to land on 8 March near Haipong. However, if the French thought that the pacification of this area would be as easily carried out as it had been in the Cochin China operations they were in for a rude awakening. In and around Hanoi and Haiphong the *Viet Minh* were well entrenched and ready to fight. Despite attempts at a peaceful settlement between the opposing forces, fighting broke out in December of 1946 at Hanoi and quickly erupted into full scale warfare between the French and the *Viet Minh*. During the initial fighting between the two sides the French came out on top, forcing the communists out of Hanoi and Haiphong, but Ho and his military leader, Nguyen Giap regrouped their forces and began carrying out guerrilla warfare against the French. In the north, as in the south, the few roads were in poor condition, and since the French forces were basically roadbound this played into the hands of the guerrillas who quickly became adept at ambushing French supply and relief columns. In an effort to counter these attacks the French Army began looking at the numerous inland waterways as a means of moving men and material. The Navy began creating a combat organization which could closely adapt itself to the peculiar conditions under which it would operate. As a result of this, a new naval formation, the *Dinassaut*, was born. In French naval terminology *Dinassaut* translated to 'Assault River Division', and, as time would show, this turned out to be one of the unique military ideas of merit to be developed by the French during the Indochina war. In the words of the noted Vietnam historian Bernard Fall, the *Dinassaut* was "...one of the few worthwhile contributions of the Indochina War to military knowledge".

The concept and structure behind these river assault divisions was quite simple, drawing in part on the experiences of Jaubert's flotilla in the south. Since the guerrillas were able to prevent the flow of supplies and impede French troop movement over what passed for a road network, the French would use the vast array of rivers and canals to move supplies, engage enemy forces, and support ground units with a reduction in risk to themselves. Obviously, *Dinassauts* could only be used where there were adequate waterways, but where these existed the French would be able to use their mobility and firepower to its fullest.

The nucleus of the *Dinassauts* was a variety of modified landing craft

* Additional information on the French in Indochina both before and after 1945 can be found in the author's ARMOR IN VIETNAM published by Squadron/Signal.

The French used landing craft in Indochina, to move troops along the waterways to avoid Viet Minh ambushes on land. This LCM has had its stern encased in armor plate and carries a number of machine guns for defense. The overhead canvas covers were for protection from the sun rather than the enemy. (Naval History Museum)

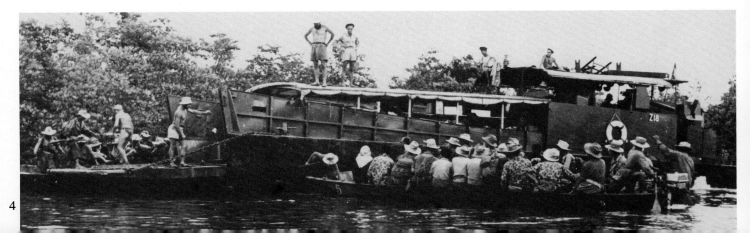

which carried a wide range of armament and protective armor. Some were used primarily in the fire support role mounting various weapons including .30 and .50 caliber machine guns, 20mm, 40mm, and 57mm cannons, and even 3 inch guns. Other craft were used mainly for troop and supply movement, but these too were armed and could provide limited fire support during operations. There were also a number of small, fast boats which were used for patrol and escort missions. The majority of these vessels were modified or converted in Vietnam and they performed exceptionally well throughout the war giving the French a valuable weapon with which to strike out against an elusive but relentless enemy.

Into Battle

The first use of the *Dinassuats* came shortly after the outbreak of open warfare in northern Vietnam. French troops in the town of Nam Dinh, southeast of Hanoi, were surrounded by a sizeable *Viet Minh* force. Realizing that an overland relief column had little chance of breaking through, the French command decided to stage a combined airborne and riverine assault on 6 January to break the siege. The plan called for paratroopers to seize two bridgeheads where the *Dinassuats* could then land their troops and supplies. Unfortunately, the airborne troops, taking heavy fire, could not secure the landing zones. The naval force, sailing up the Red River, were caught in a vicious crossfire which killed the unit's commander and sank one boat. Undaunted, the executive officer landed his troops opposite the planned beachhead, and backed up with fire from his remaining landing craft cleared the area of enemy. Once this area was seized, fire was switched to the opposite shore. Within a short time, this fire drove the *Viet Minh* from their positions and the French troops were able to secure the beachhead. This broke the back of the *Viet Minh*, and by noon the relief force had entered the city. However, even with the arrival of these relief forces, the town remained under the gun. The *Viet Minh* continued to hold the surrounding countryside and for a long time afterwards *Dinassuats* provided the only means of getting supplies and reinforcements to the town.

The next major employment of the *Dinassuats* came during OPERATION LEA, launched in October of 1947 to capture the top *Viet Minh* leadership and destroy supply depots in the Viet Bac region. This combined air-ground-river assault included a drive by *Dinassuat* units up the Red and Clear River valleys in northwestern Tonkin. Unfortunately, LEA did not reap the benefits the French had hoped it would. And while all objectives were seized and over 9000 enemy soldiers were reported killed, Ho Chi Minh and his subordinates managed to escape the trap. The naval forces, after experiencing problems with sand bars, reached their objectives but not before the bulk of the guerrillas had slipped away into the surrounding jungle. However, the

performance of naval forces impressed the army, and in the future they would use the *Dinassuats* whenever possible.

Throughout the remainder of the late 40s the French Army tried to force the elusive *Viet Minh* into a set piece battle where they could bring their superior firepower against Ho Chi Minh's guerrilla army. But Ho and Giap resisted such traps and waged a hit and run war, striking isolated outposts or small convoys where they could mount overwhelming numbers and then disappear before the French could react. However this all changed in late 1950 when Giap launched a massive assault against French garrisons along the Chinese-Vietnamese border. Everyone of them fell to the guerrillas, except Mon Cay, near the coast where French ships were able to effectively support the position and bring in supplies by sea.

Undeterred by this single failure Giap reorganized his forces and prepared to strike at Hanoi and Haiphong. The French, who had just received massive amounts of military aid from the United States, used the lull to prepare for the anticipated attack. In particular new landing craft allowed the navy to form two additional *dinassauts* which reinforced the two already in the Tonkin region. On 13 January 1951 the long expected assault came. *Viet Minh* troops poured out of the hills, attacking the strategic town of Vinh Yen on the fringe of the Red River delta about forty miles northwest of Hanoi. The new French commander, General Jean de Lattre de Tassigny, responded with all available air, ground, and riverine units. *Dinassaut* units carried troops up the Red River and landed them near Vinh Yen to reinforce the

(Above) These small French craft were FOM (short) support boats which was the abbreviation for France Outre Mer. This designation was given to the class because the boats were made for overseas use. They were one of the few boats that the French designed especially for use on the rivers of Indochina. (Naval History Museum)

(Below) This LCM has been turned into a 'Monitor' with the addition of a turret from a Coventry armored car on its bow; machine guns have also been added to the stern. The crows nest provided a good vantage point from which to spot mines or possible ambushes, but if the observer was caught there during a firefight his life expectancy was rather short. (Naval History Museum)

town's beleaguered defenders. Together with the Army and Air Force, the Naval Forces helped inflict over 6,000 casualties on Giap's troops before the attack was called off.

Chafing at this defeat, Giap withdrew to mend his wounds. Two months later, on 23 March he launched another attack, this time aimed at Mao Khe, twenty miles north of Haiphong. Located near the Da Bach river, this small town was garrisoned by only 400 men. Against them Giap threw nearly three divisions, the 308th, 312th, and 316th. During the first assault, the communists succeeded in overwhelming almost all outer defensive positions. By the 26th, the situation at Mao Khe was critical, but fortunately three French destroyers and two LSSLs were able to enter the deep bay of the Da Bach River and provide much needed fire support. They also covered the landing of a paratrooper battalion and naval commandos who reinforced the nearly exhausted troops at Mao Khe. Coupled with massive air support, this effort saved the town and drove off the *Viet Minh* who left behind over 400 dead. This naval support played a vital role in the defense of Mao Khe when it broke up a large concentration of *Viet Minh* troops who were massing for a final assault against the last remaining defensive position. Had this force not been dispersed, the town would undoubtedly have fallen.

Despite these successive setbacks, Giap launched yet a third attack, but this time shifted the assault to French positions south of Haiphong. On 28 May, over 40,000 *Viet Minh* troops struck the French line along the Day River southwest of Nam Dinh. A key objective of this drive was the town of Ninh Binh whose capture was assigned to the 308th Division. The initial attack caught the defenders, a Marine Commando unit by surprise and most of the

town was captured. The next day, *Dinassaut 3*, loaded with reinforcements, sailed from Nam Dinh to rescue the few remaining Marines. Despite being caught in an ambush eight miles from the town which damaged a number of the landing craft, the *Dinassaut* fought its way through the trap and reached the town. With these reinforcements the defenders were able to hold out. In the meantime the *Dinassaut* began attacking *Viet Minh* positions along the waters edge and naval commandos who reinforced the nearly exhausted troops at Mao Khe. As additional *Viet Minh* troops poured into the area two temporary *Dinassauts*, organized from landing craft found in Hanoi, were thrown into the battle. The battle raged on for days around Ninh Binh and finally reaching a climax in the fight for Yen Cu Ha, a key outpost south of the main French position. The fighting seesawed back and forth until support fire from an LSSL finally broke the back of the enemy's resistance. Sporadic fighting continued for a few more days but the *Viet Minh* had had enough. By 18 June, Giap had pulled his troops back across the Day River and called off the operation.

After this battering, Giap called a halt to offensive operations and withdrew to regroup and rest his troops. Taking advantage of this respite General de Lattre decided to go on the offensive, and in mid-November launched OPERATION LOTUS to capture the town of Hoa Binh, located on the Black River, and cut the *Viet Minh* supply lines to their forces south of the delta. On 14 November paratroopers seized Hoa Binh while a ground column pushed down from Hanoi along Route 6 to link up with them. The initial phase of the battle went very well for the French with little opposition being encountered. However, once the town was taken, keeping it supplied became

(Below) An LCM nudges up to the shore to unload supplies during an operation in Cochin China's Plain of Reeds. Note how the aft end of the vessel bristles with machine guns. (Naval History Museum)

These fast patrol boats were armed with a .50 caliber machine gun and a 20mm cannon. During the battle of Hoa Binh these craft suffered heavy losses when they tried to escort landing craft through a Viet Minh blockade near Notre Dame Rock. (Naval History Museum)

(Below) A FOM(long) support boat slowly moves along a narrow waterway during a patrol in the Mekong Delta. Its manned by a mixed French and Vietnamese crew which was common late in the war as the French tried to solve their manpower shortage by the recruiting and training of local troops. (Naval History Museum)

a nightmare since the French could not continuously keep Route 6 open. To keep the town supplied, the Black River became the main supply line along which the French moved men and materials. French Navy officers, involved in the planning of LOTUS, had pointed out that although the river was navigable for the *Dinassauts* it was also ideal for ambushes. Despite these warnings the Army commanders did not feel this was a major problem and counted on the river as the main supply route.

Giap, however, realized just how vulnerable these river convoys were and focused his main attacks against them in the hopes of starving out the defenders at Hoa Binh. Throughout December he whittled away at French positions along the river and harassed the *Dinassauts* as they tried to keep open the lines of communications. By mid-January 1952 Giap was ready to close the river to the French. On 12 January, a convoy was ambushed south of Notre Dame Rock. Previously the *Dinassauts* had been able to fight their way through to Hoa Binh, but this time the guerrillas were too strong. Heavy fire from the shore severely damaged most of the landing craft despite the valiant efforts of their escorts. Closing to almost point blank range the escorts paid a fearful price for their bravery. Four patrol boats and one heavily armed LSSL were sunk before the convoy commander gave up and ordered the force back to its base. After this defeat, further efforts to supply Hoa Binh using river convoys was abandoned.

General de Lattre, dying from cancer, was relieved by General Raoul Salan, who decided that Hoa Binh was not worth the cost of holding it. As a result, he ordered it evacuated. Unfortunately two LCMs trapped upriver by low water, were lost during the withdrawal, one was sunk by enemy fire while the other was scuttled by its crew to keep it out of enemy hands.

Throughout the spring and summer of 1952, both sides carried out limited attacks on each other, but for the most part the time was spent consolidating their respective positions. In October Giap launched an offensive against French positions in the T'ai Highlands of northwest Tonkin between the Red and Black Rivers. These outposts, deep in the interior, were quickly overrun. None were near a waterway and as a result no *Dinassuat* could support them as had been the case in Giap's earlier assaults. The lack of riverine support effectively doomed these French positions even before the *Viet Minh* launched their attacks.

To counter these attacks, Salan initiated OPERATION LORRAINE, the largest offensive yet carried out by the French in Indochina. Its main purpose was to disrupt the flow of supplies to the Viet Minh from China and take pressure off French forces in the T'ai Highlands. From the outset, the *Dinassauts* played an important part in the campaign. In preparation for LORRAINE they ferried troops and equipment to staging areas at Trung Ha on the Red River and Viet Tri on the Clear River. On 29 October, after helping to ferry Army units across the waterway, the *Dinassauts* moved up the Red River toward Phu Tho. On the Clear River, naval units pushed north from Viet Tri and joined forces with those moving up from Trung Ho. This link up took place just north of Phu Tho at Ngoc Thap. From there the two columns sailed toward Phu Doan, a major *Viet Minh* supply base at the juncture of the Clear and Chay Rivers. After Phu Doan was captured against only token resistance, patrols pushed on to Phu Yen Binh. Throughout the operation the *Dinassauts* moved up the various waterways covering the Army units

(Below) These patrol craft make a high speed sweep in hopes of catching the guerrillas making a supply run. While fast, these boats were lightly armored and could not stand up to the heavy fire usually encountered in an ambush. (Naval History Museum)

(Below) A FOM(short) support boat is part of a river convoy escort along with a Grumman Goose. The main difference besides length between the two FOM classes (short and long) was the additional gun turret mounted aft on the long model. (Naval History Museum)

(Below) Armored French LCVPs were used as escorts for river convoys and in search missions against guerrilla forces. These craft have a 20mm cannon mounted in a forward turret and carry a number of .30 and .50 caliber machine guns along the sides. The pointed bow added to the landing door was to aid the boat in extracting itself from the shoreline after beaching. (Naval History Museum)

(Below) A patrol boat hails a freighter for inspection of its cargo. On occasion the Viet Minh used commercial vessels to smuggle weapons into the country. (Naval History Museum)

The crew of this LCM maneuvers their craft along a narrow waterway in the Red River Delta. In such confined space a Viet Minh ambush could be deadly and the French had to always be on the alert. (Naval History Museum)

Shallow drafted vessels such as this Patrol Escort (PCE) were often employed by the French in the deep water bays of northern Vietnam where they could bring heavy firepower to bear on the enemy. During the battle of Mao Khe this kind of support saved the town and inflicted heavy casualties on the attacking communist forces. (Naval History Museum)

Deep water bays also allowed the French to bring their carriers in close to cut down the distance that their aircraft had to fly to the target. The carrier LaFayette (ex-USS Langley CVL-27) sails into picturesque Along Bay in support of French troops in the Red River Delta. (Naval History Museum)

marching overland. Often they embarked infantry units to pursue guerrillas who had slipped away from the ground columns. In addition they also protected the flanks of the Army drive and kept it resupplied. However, in spite of all this support, LORRAINE failed to take pressure off the French in the T'ai region. While the operation did temporarily disrupt the *Viet Minh's* supply lines and resulted in the capture of numerous supply dumps, Giap was able to keep pressure on French troops in the T'ai region. He realized that the French, in carrying out this operation, had overextended themselves, and it was only a matter of time until the French were forced to pull back. By mid-November Salan ordered both his ground troops and naval units to pull back.

Following LORRAINE, large scale military operations by both sides tapered off sharply. During this period both combatants recouped their losses and tried to consolidate their positions. In April of 1953 a new French commander, General Henri Navarre, took over from General Salan. His arrival coincided with another influx of American aid and Navarre staged local counterattacks so he could further consolidate his positions. After which, he planned to entice the *Viet Minh* into a final set piece battle and destroy their military power. Coinciding with Navarre's arrival and due in part to the additional equipment supplied by the US, and to the desire of the French to supplement their forces with local units, the first Vietnamese *Dinassaut* was activated in the Mekong Delta. During this period the *Viet Minh* renewed their offensive, moving into Laos which caused Navarre to move in troops to contain the assault. Due to the lack of navigatable waterways the *Dinassauts* played no part in this campaign.

In late October, Giap struck at Phu Ly on the Day River with the 320th Division. Navarre responded with OPERATION MOVETTE, moving several mobile units into the area aboard the boats of *Dinassauts 3* and *12*, while other units moved on Phu Nho, the supply depot for the 320th. Heavy fighting erupted, but neither side could gain the upper hand. Navarre, rather than pour in additional forces, called off the French drive and withdrew his troops to regroup for a new offensive. On 20 November, French paratroopers descended on the small village of Dien Bien Phu in northwestern Tonkin. Over the next few months more men and equipment were brought in and the position was heavily fortified. However, isolated from the main French positions in the Red River Valley by hundreds of miles of trackless jungle and mountains, Dien Ben Phu could only be supplied by air. Confident in his men, equipment and the steps taken to fortify the position, Navarre hoped that by presenting Giap with such a tempting target he could lure the communist general into committing his main combat units into a final set piece battle that the French had sought for so long. Unfortunately for the French it was a fatal mistake. Giap's infantry had carried artillery and anti-aircraft guns through the jungle and across mountains, and used them to pound the fortress's airstrip and all but stopped the flow of supplies. Despite heroic resistance the position fell in May of 1954, the day before the start of peace talks in Geneva between the two combatants. This defeat marked the end of French rule in Indochina. Though negotiations dragged on for three months, for all intents and purposes the loss of Dien Bien Phu marked the end of the first Indochina War.

Naval Air and Surface Support

While the main thrust of French naval activities centered around the *Dinassauts*, air and surface forces also played a vital role in the war. In the early stages of the campaign, surface ships provided fire support and augmented forces ashore with detachments of marines and sailors when the need arose. In particular the town of Nha Trang, surrounded by *Viet Minh* forces, relied on ships for supplies and support prior to the outbreak of open warfare between the two sides.

French cruisers and destroyers provided valuable fire support in the battle for Tourane*. And once it was recaptured, these same ships supported a number of amphibious landings along the coast to secure Hue and the Fai Fo region during early 1947. The landings at Fai Fo marked the first combat use of carrier aircraft by the French when the 12,850t escort carrier Dixmude (formerly the HMS Biter), launched Douglas SDB Dauntless dive bombers to support the landings. For two weeks the carrier stayed in the area, providing air support for the troops ashore. Dixmude then moved north toward Haiphong, hitting *Viet Minh* targets northwest of Hanoi. These actions, though small in nature, underlined the ability of the aircraft carrier to project airpower over a wide area. And since airfields were few and far between in Indochina, the aircraft carrier proved particularly valuable and the French came to rely more and more upon carrier based aircraft as the war went on.

Prior to this the only naval aircraft to see service in the war zone were PBY Catalinas and Grumman JRF Gooses. In late October of 1945, six PBY-5As of the *8th Flotilla (Escadrille 8F)* arrived at Tan Son Nhut. Almost immediately they began flying surveillance missions along the coast and over the Mekong Delta. In February of 1946, the squadron, strengthened with additional aircraft, moved to the Hanoi-Haiphong area to reinforce forces there. Following the outbreak of war in December, they were pressed into service as transports, moving troops around the Tonkin Gulf area to counter *Viet Minh* attacks. Once the situation stabilized, the PBYs again took up their regular patrol work flying long missions up and down the coast to prevent enemy infiltration of arms by sea. During OPERATION LEA PBYs flew long range reconnaissance and even ground support missions for the army, sometimes operating at tree top level. Unfortunately, such activities did not suit the large slow flying boat, and after taking losses the 'Cats' were pulled out of the ground support role.

The Grumman JRF Goose, a small twin engine amphibian was used mainly in the central and southern portions of Indochina for liaison, surveillance, casualty evacuation, and ground support. Fitted with machine guns and bomb racks the Goose often provided air cover for *Dinassaut* operations or amphibious landings. They played a particularly important role during OPERATION ATLANTE, an amphibious assault carried out against *Viet Minh* forces north of Nha Trang near Tuy Hoa. On occasion, the Goose also provided support to army units inland. During the siege of Dak Doa in the central highlands the Goose supported elements of *GM 100* until the *Viet Minh* succeeded in overwhelming the small garrison. Unlike the Catalina, which was replaced in the early 1950s, the Goose was used until the end of hostilities in 1954.

While the Catalina had performed well during their deployment, the French needed a more modern aircraft for coastal surveillance. In 1949, they requested PB4Y Privateers from a US military mission visiting Indochina**. This was eventually granted, and in late 1950 ten Privateers arrived at Tan Son Nhut replacing the PBYs of the *8th Flotilla*. Almost immediately they were pressed into service as heavy bombers to aid French forces around Vinh Yen during Giap's first offensive. From then on the Privateers were more often used as heavy bombers than patrol aircraft. In particular the PB4Y's long range and endurance allowed them to be used for attacks deep in enemy territory and as flare ships that could loiter over embattled positions at night. Often two plane detachments were sent out to other airfields for broader

Later renamed Da Nang.

**Naval patrol version of the B-24 Liberator bomber.*

(Below) This Grumman Goose has been pressed into the casualty evacuation role. Other JRFs were fitted with bomb racks and used to support riverine units. Some even served as flare ships during night operations. (ECPA via Camelio)

coverage of a battlefield. During the siege of Dien Bien Phu, Privateers began bombing Viet Minh supply dumps and depots. They also hit anti-aircraft and artillery positions close to the fortifications in an attempt to silence the enemy guns, but low hanging clouds and dense jungle combined to hamper the effectiveness of these bombing attacks. As the siege dragged on additional PB4Ys were sent out to replace losses and to form an additional unit, the *28th Flotilla*. Before these new aircraft could be effectively committed, Dien Bien Phu fell. Ironically the last aircraft lost over Dien Bien Phu was a Privateer which was shot down on the night the fortress surrendered.

Following the success of the Dixmude the French deployed another carrier, the 18,040t Arromanches (formerly the British light carrier Colossus). In late 1948 Arromanches began supporting ground operations with her Dauntless and Seafire aircraft. In less than two months aircraft off Arromanches flew more sorties than the French Air Force did throughout 1948. Unfortunately the carrier could not be kept on station indefinitely and she was pulled out in January of 1949. Twenty months later, in September of 1951, Aeromanches returned, this time with more modern F6F Hellcats and SB2C Helldivers. During a seven month tour, her air group flew over 1,400 sorties, a considerable number when the whole aircraft complement aboard totaled only forty-four machines. Many of these sorties were flown in support of French naval and ground units taking part in the fighting around Hoa Binh. After this deployment the Arromanches returned to France but was again off the coast of Indochina in October of 1953, just in time to provide support for OPERATION LORRAINE.

The outstanding job done by both the Dixmude and Arromanches prompted the French to seek another carrier for use in Indochina. In 1951 the 10,662t light carrier La Fayette (ex-USS Langley) was acquired. She relieved Arromanches in early 1953 and flew numerous sorties until forced to enter drydock for an overhaul. Her relief was none other than the Arromanches which perhaps fittingly helped close the naval air war over Indochina. Her aircrews took part in the climactic struggle at Dien Bien Phu where they flew countless sorties in support of the hardpressed defenders. During the siege Arromanches' two squadrons were so decimated that they had to be withdrawn from operations, being replaced by aircrews off the 10,662t light carrier Bois Belleau (ex-USS Belleau Wood) flying F4U Corsairs. But these reinforcements could do little to turn the tide and Dien Bien Phu fell. French naval aviators performed valiantly during the siege as they aided their hardpressed comrades on the ground. Unfortunately their gallant efforts could do little in the face of the tactical mistake of the French military leadership that placed their troops in such an inaccessible position.

(Above) The only long strategic bomber the French had were Aeronavale PB4Y Privateers. These Privateers of the 28th Flotilla are being prepared for a mission at Cat Bi airfield near Hanoi. (ECPA via Camelio)

The Vietnamese Navy

The Early Years

The foundations of the Vietnamese Navy were laid down in late 1949 when the French, because of a manpower shortage, decided to develop the armed forces of Vietnam. In the original proposal only a 'river navy' was envisioned in Indochina by French authorities, but a later plan drafted in Paris also called for a limited number of ocean going ships. In April of 1951, based on proposals from both the theater commander and Paris authorities, a four year program was adopted. Included in this joint proposal were plans for several river flotillas, eight minesweepers, two naval assault divisions, a corvette, two escorts, and a naval training center. Despite these lofty plans, little was initially done to implement them. French field commanders who had been recruiting Vietnamese for their own needs felt that if a strong effort was made to build up a Vietnamese Navy, they would not have the manpower to fill their own thin ranks.

It was not until 1953 that the first Vietnamese naval force was activated. On 10 April a small *Dinassaut* unit of five landing craft was organized for operations in the Mekong Delta. They were based at Can Tho, and although they flew the Vietnamese flag, the craft were under French command and partially manned by French sailors. A second *Dinassaut* unit was formed

During the spring of 1953 the French activated the first Vietnamese naval units in the Mekong Delta. These 'Vietnamese units' were made up of Vietnamese personnel under the command of French officers. This LCVP being towed by another craft is taking part in a patrol near Can Tho. Note that the craft flies both the French and Vietnamese flags. Initially there was a dispute between the two countries as to which flag the vessels would fly causing a delay in the turnover of additional boats to the Vietnamese. (Naval History Division)

Once the French agreed to withdrawal from Indochina a large number of the landing craft, patrol boats, and other miscellaneous vessels of the Dinassauts were turned over to the fledgeling Vietnamese Navy. Seen here are three 'Vendettes', one of the few specially built craft which the French used for their river operations. Once the French severed their ties with the South Vietnamese these vessels had to be retired due to a lack of spare parts. (Naval History Museum)

later that summer at Vinh Long to patrol the Mekong River where it flowed into the sea. After this second unit was formed, a delay arose in expansion while French and Vietnamese military bureaucrats argued over which flag the vessels would fly. Once this was cleared up, the expansion of the Vietnamese Navy continued. In January of 1954, three minesweepers were turned over to Vietnamese control, and was followed by the formation of two more *Dinassaut* units in March and August.

In northern Vietnam French forces were locked in the bitter struggle with *Viet Minh* troops at Dien Bien Phu. This defeat took the heart out of French resistance and had a profound effect on the peace talks which started at Geneva the next day. Eventually the talks resulted in an agreement which called for the withdrawal of French troops, and a *temporary partition* of the country until a nation-wide election could take place. Though the French were bound by the accord to pull out, the agreement allowed for an orderly transition of power. But since the treaty did not include either the US or the new government formed in the south of Vietnam by Ngo Diem, neither felt bound to abide by the terms of the treaty. American and French authorities worked out an agreement with Diem whereby US advisors would gradually replace French personnel and train the Vietnamese armed forces.

For a short period of time both French and US naval personnel worked side by side in a combined training mission known as the Training Relations Instruction Mission (TRIM). However, by the fall of 1955 US advisors had taken over most of these duties, although, the last French advisor did not leave Vietnam until May of 1957. The naval force which TRIM personnel worked with was relatively small, numbering only some 2000 officers and men. Its modest equipment included two LSMs, two PCEs, three MSCs, and about 200 landing craft, plus some miscellaneous smaller craft. After analyzing the military requirements which might be placed upon the Vietnamese naval forces, the US advisors came up with the following list of possible mission requirements: amphibious operations, river and coastal patrol, minesweeping, fire support, and logistic support. Obviously, such tasks were far beyond current Vietnamese naval training and equipment. But, such a force was obviously needed if South Vietnam was to have the ability to protect its newly declared independence. US advisors immediately began working to build up this naval force as outlined in the analysis.

Unfortunately, problems arose almost at once which hindered this expansion as religious and criminal groups rebelled against Diem's rule. Among these were the *Cao Dai* religious sect near Tay Ninh, the *Hoa Hao* paramilitary religious group around Can Tho, and the *Binh Xuyen* criminal organization in the Saigon-Cholon area. After taking control of Saigon from the *Binh Xuyen* in May of 1955, Diem next struck at the *Hoa Hao* during June. Using almost all of the small Vietnamese Navy to move troops and provide support, Diem attacked the *Hoa Hao* in the Can Tho area. By the end of the month *Hoa Hao* resistance had been crushed around the city, although some units were able to escape during the fighting into the swamps around the town.

On 1 July 1955, overall command of the Vietnamese Navy passed out of French hands, and the new Vietnamese commander was almost immediately called upon to provide support for another major operation. When Diem had taken control of Saigon and defeated the *Binh Xuyen*, hard core members of the organization had fled to the Rung Sat swamp south of Saigon. This area, consisting of over 300 square miles of waterways and mangrove covered swampland, served as a base from which the *Binh Xuyen* carried out terrorist attacks and raids against shipping. In September Diem decided to destroy the

This 'Vedette' patrol boat has been drydocked for repairs. These craft became the main patrol boat of the Vietnamese River Assault Groups (RAGs) until replaced by newer American equipment in the 1960s. These vessels were nicknamed 'Rag Boats' after the Vietnamese units using them. (US Navy via Cressman)

power of the *Binh Xuyen* once and for all. During the middle of the month naval units blocked off the region and began bombarding shore positions. While numbering only some 1,500 men, the *Binh Xuyen* was well equipped with small arms, mortars, bazookas, machine guns, and recoilless rifles. Even after this initial assault, the *Binh Xuyen* showed no inclination to surrender, so on 21 September the Vietnamese launched a combined assault with all four *Dinassauts* supporting Army and Navy troops. While the *Dinassauts* blocked their escape along the waterways, ground troops gradually forced the *Binh Xuyen* into an ever tightening pocket. Faced with annihilation, the surviving *Binh Xuyen* troops surrendered. US advisors, observing for the first time Vietnamese naval units in action, were impressed with what they saw. And while problems did crop up, Vietnamese naval personnel carried out their assignments quickly and efficiently. Overall success of the operation was due to the ability of the *Dinassauts* to transport troops to positions in the Rung Sat Swamp and then act as a blocking force to prevent the enemy from escaping.

After this operation in the Rung Sat swamp, only splinter groups of the *Cao Dai* and remnants of the *Hoa Hao* sects still posed any problem to the Diem government. In November two *Dinassaut* units helped the Army of the Republic of Vietnam (ARVN) troops isolate the *Hoa Hao* at Rach Gia on the Gulf of Siam, while along the Mekong River other naval units fought pitched battles with *Hoa Hao* troops who were being aided by *Viet Minh* advisors. North of Saigon, the *Soar* faction of the *Hoa Hao* sect, operating out of the Plain of Reeds, continued to resist all efforts by ARVN troops to subdue them. However, with the help of the *Dinassauts*, ARVN troops were finally able to exert enough pressure to force this group to come into the Diem government in February of 1956. Once this faction fell into line, government forces in the area were able to shift their attention back to Rach Gia. With the aid of all four *Dinassauts*, government troops pressed in on the dissidents around the town. During April the leader of the faction was captured and *Hoa Hao* resistance collapsed.

After this extensive campaign the job of subduing the *Cao Daists* was relatively mild in comparison. Vietnamese naval units provided only limited support as ARVN troops captured the sect's capital at Tay Ninh. This forced their leader to flee and, with him gone, the sect worked out an agreement with Diem whereby their religion was legalized and they in turn would support the Diem government. This ended the last organized resistance from these three groups, although a few small bands continued to be a nuisance for a period of time afterwards.

At the beginning of 1956, the Vietnamese Navy organized some of their larger ships into an ocean going Sea Force. Two main naval posts were set up, one at the southern tip, and the other near the Demilitarized Zone (DMZ). Five Sea Zones were set up and the Vietnamese began patrolling their long coastline. Unfortunately, there were not nearly enough ships for this job and the Vietnamese proposed to their US advisors that a fleet of fifty 14t motorized junks be organized to supplement the existing naval units. However it was not until the early 1960's that steps were taken to implement this plan.

Shortly after the formation of the Sea Force it was called upon to protect Vietnamese interests in the Paracels and Spratly Islands, located 200 miles east of Da Nang. These islands were claimed by Vietnam, Nationalist China, Communist China, and the Philippines. In June reports indicated that Chinese Communist forces had landed in the Paracels. To counter this the Vietnamese dispatched a PC, an LSM, two LSILs, and a territorial company of troops to garrison and patrol the area. No action resulted from this movement of forces and the Vietnamese continued to garrison the islands throughout the 1950s.

In other areas, the Vietnamese Navy also expanded its scope of operations. During the fall of 1956 it began patrols out of Da Nang to stop communist infiltration from the sea. The number of *Dinassauts* were increased to six with bases at My Tho, Cat Lo, Vinh Long, Cat Lai, Can Tho, and Long Xuyen. At Dong Ha, near the DMZ, a small base was set up from which utility boats could carry out inshore patrols along the coast just south of the Zone. Further south, in the Gulf of Siam, naval units carried out training and patrol operations in response to supposed Cambodian seizures of Vietnamese fishing boats. All these actions, though minor, combined to give the fledgling Vietnamese Navy confidence in itself and valuable training as full scale war approached the tiny nation.

(Right) The Vietnamese also converted a few LCMs to Command Communications Boats (CCBs). This CCB has a 20mm cannon in the bow turret and several mounts on the stern for either .30 or .50 caliber machine guns. (US Navy)

(Above) An armed LCVP departs its base on a patrol along the My Tho river. This craft, though modified by the French, was of American origin and, with the arrival of US Navy advisors, formed the basis of the early Brown Water units which tried to contain the rising threat of the Viet Cong. (US Navy)

(Below) A French modified American LCM which the Vietnamese inherited. Since many of the French riverine craft were originally American landing craft, spare parts were no problem once the United States began supplying aid to the Diem regime. (US Navy)

The Vietnamese modified a number of LCMs for use as fire support boats known as 'Monitors', and while of the same general design, each individual boat varied in detail and armament. Each of these three Monitors differ from each other in several ways. The top one mounts a 37mm turret from a M-8 armored car and has a flat bow. The middle Monitor has a pointed bow with a specially designed 40mm turret and a different stern configuration than either of the others. The bottom Monitor, though fitted with the same flat bow as the top Monitor, carries the specially designed 40mm turret. The 40mm turret used on the middle and bottom LCMs would eventually become the standard armament on future Vietnamese Monitors and in a modified form would also be used by US riverine forces. (US Navy)

Conflict With North Vietnam

By mid-1957, it had become obvious to Ho Chi Minh that any hope of a unified Vietnam under his leadership (i.e. communist rule) would only be brought about by force. President Diem had successfully consolidated his power and established a pro-western government in the south. The communists immediately began a campaign of terror and violence against Diem's rule. In particular, a great deal of this activity took place in the Mekong Delta southwest of Saigon. Because there were few roads in this swampy delta region, the Navy was called upon to provide support and transportation for ARVN troops as they fought against the communists. The Navy proved extremely effective in the Mekong and registered a number of successes in the fighting. The *Dinassauts* had been renamed in the interim, now being called River Assault Groups (RAGs). Unfortunately this initial employment of the RAGs against the communists highlighted a problem which was to be a constant source of irritation to the Vietnamese Navy. During these operations Navy units came under the control of local Army commanders who were usually unfamiliar with naval tactics and problems; Naval considerations such as tides, limited maneuvering room, shallow water, and water obstructions, were seldom taken into account by Army commanders when planning operations that included riverine units. A great deal of animosity was created when Naval personnel tried to explain these problems to the Army, or when a Naval force failed to carry out an assigned task because of one of these problems. Educating the Army to naval limitations was to be a constant and on going problem for the Navy throughout the war.

In response to an increase in communist activity modest steps began in 1960 to expand and modernize the Vietnamese Navy. The Navy Section of the US Military Assistance Advisory Group (MAAG) was increased to a strength of sixty men to help with this expansion. Unfortunately the program resulted in only a marginal increase in Vietnamese naval personnel, most of whom were assigned to shore establishments, which were becoming disproportionately large in relation to the operational forces they supported. Even worse, some Vietnamese commanders began padding their payroll with false names and siphoning off the money to their own private accounts. Some new equipment, primarily patrol craft, were received, but the largest increase in ships took place within the Junk Force, a paramilitary unit composed mainly of civilians under Navy officers.

By the end of 1961, it was apparent to US officials in Vietnam that the expanding war being waged by the communists against Diem would require more American advisors, aid, and possibly limited help by US operational units. Almost immediately US minesweepers (MSOs) began operating with

Some LCVPs were lightly armored for use in transporting personnel and carried only a few machine guns for defense. These boats were not intended for use in river operations. This particular boat is carrying General Westmoreland, the US Commander in Vietnam and General Tran Ngoc Tam, Commanding General of Vietnamese Regional Forces, on a tour of the River Defense Training Center at Saigon. (US Navy)

Thirty-six LCVPs were fitted with armor and machine guns for use by the Civil Guard River Patrol on the smaller rivers and canals in the Mekong Delta. This civilian defense unit was used to supplement regular naval forces but unfortunately the lack of funds, training, equipment, and repair facilities severely hampered the unit and it never really became an effective fighting force. (US Navy)

Vietnamese Naval units near the DMZ on 'barier' patrols in an attempt to cut down communist infiltration by sea. In February of 1962, these patrols were expanded when American destroyer escorts (DEs) began similiar operations near the Can Mau peninsula. These American units were not allowed to engage targets, but used their radar to vector Vietnamese craft to suspicious targets. These patrols were suspended in late spring when little evidence of large scale infiltration was discovered.

In conjunction with this initial deployment of US ships to work with the Vietnamese Navy, the number of US advisors assigned to the RAGs, the Junk Forces, the Sea Force, and shore facilities increased dramatically. The expansion of all aspects of the US aid program in Vietnam resulted in the establishment of the Military Assistance Command, Vietnam (MACV) in February of 1962, and the formation of the Headquarters Support Activity in July.

However, even with this increase in American commitment to the war, the situation continued to deteriorate for the Vietnamese Armed Forces. Promotion in the Army by political influence rather than ability severly hurt leadership; and while rampant corruption enriched the higher ranks, it virtually deprived the enlisted ranks the means to sustain their families. These problems caused a drop in Army morale and a consequent lack of motivation in the field. The Navy was not immune to corruption, and because the Navy offered smaller risks, many of the richer city dwellers bribed their way into it. As a result of these and other problems an official fact finding team under General Maxwell Taylor arrived in Vietnam during October of 1962, to assess the US and South Vietnamese war effort. From General Taylor's observations came recommendations to increase US aid and support. Project 'Beef-Up' was set in motion; more advisors, equipment and money were sent to prop up Diem. In addition, operational participation of US forces was increased substantially.

However, 'Beef-Up' could not reverse the faltering South Vietnamese government. Plagued by political turmoil, Diem became even more repressive in dealing with his opposition. In November of 1963, this led to his overthrow and murder by dissident army troops. Diem's demise did little to stabilize the situation. The succession of civilian and military governments which followed Diem's ousting were unable to marshall public support, nor were they able to effectively prosecute the war.

During this time frame the performance of the Vietnamese Navy fell drastically. In early 1964 it had a strength of over 6,000 men, who manned fifty patrol craft and minesweepers, along with over 200 riverine and amphibious craft, but its contribution to the war effort was minimal. Rarely were the RAGs, Sea Force, or Junk units able to field at more than fifty per cent of their strength. And even these operational figures were suspect, since operational sortie figures were usually padded with administrative and supply trips. The over 700 US advisors who worked with these units voiced complaints, but little was done to alleviate the situation by the Vietnamese Command. In particular, the Junk Force faced sever problems. Seriously undermanned, much of its manpower was aged or infirmed men who had been forced into the Junk Force by poverty or the loss of their livelyhood by the war. And while the Junk Force was given the responsibility for curbing the seaborne infiltration of men and arms by the communists, it was ill prepared to effectively carry out its mission.

The infiltration problem was investigated by MACV naval officers and reported on in early 1964. This report indicated that the increased level of infiltration by the North Vietnamese, using junks and trawlers along the coast, was sufficient to support the expanding guerrilla war being carried out against the government of South Vietnam. The report also stated that little was being done to stem this flow by South Vietnamese naval units, and recommended that US naval units augment South Vietnamese patrols, but pointed out that this would achieve only partial results unless steps were also implemented to block inland infiltration routes. Lastly, it advised that a force needed to be created for deployment in the Mekong Delta to prevent *Viet Cong* (VC) infiltration and supply movements in this region.

While this report was being evaluated, the posture of the war changed dramatically. In May of 1964 MACV absorbed the old MAAG organization. Construction of new naval facilities were started at various ports along the coast, and new river patrol craft (RPC) designs were evaluated and ordered. Then, in August, American destroyers on patrol in the Gulf of Tonkin were attacked by North Vietnamese PT boats. In response to this attack the Congress of the United States passed the 'Gulf of Tonkin Resolution' which effectively gave President Johnson the power to wage war across the entire length and breadth of North and South Vietnam. The stage was now set for American naval forces to take an active role against the communist forces.

The Vietnamese also obtained a number of vessels which could be used for coastal patrol and had a shallow enough draft to also be used on the rivers. Long Dao (HQ 327) is an Infantry Landing Ship (Large) (LSIL) which saw service with the US Navy as the LSIL 698 and the French as LSIL 9029. Due to the age of many of these vessels spare parts were hard to come by and they were often out of commission. (US Navy via Cressman)

Nguyen Doc Bong (HQ-231) a Support Landing Ship (Large) (LSSL), sits at anchor on the Bassac river south of Saigon. This ship formerly served with the US Navy as LSSL 129. It is armed with a 3 inch gun in the bow, a pair of twin 40mm turrets fore and aft, plus a number of 20mm cannons. These boats could provide a high volume of fire during an engagement and their relatively shallow draft enabled them to support Vietnamese forces both along the coast and far up major rivers. (US Navy via Cressman)

During the early 1960s the South Vietnamese attempted to augment their naval forces with a coastal junk force manned by local civilian defense forces. However, the initial attempt failed to achieve meaningful results due to the caliber of manpower and the lack of initiative on the part of regular navy personnel assigned to the project. This, along with corruption and old equipment seriously hampered the force's effectiveness until more modern junks were procured and the status of the force was raised. This junk returns with troops after a fruitless search mission looking for Viet Cong troops. (US Navy)

Small RAG boats carried both .30 and .50 caliber machine guns but were lightly armored and could not stand up to fire from a well executed communist ambush. This craft cruises along a canal which bisects a small village in the Ca Mau peninsula. Often these Vietnamese Navy patrol boats were the only contact villages deep in the Delta had with the central government. (US Navy)

This LCM waits for the tide to go out before it can proceed under the bridge in the foreground. Such problems were often encountered during riverine operations, but the Navy found it difficult to convince the Army that such things had to be considered when planning a joint mission against the VC. (US Army)

(Below) Linh Kiem (HQ-226) patrols along the lower reaches of the Long Tau River near the Rung Sat Special Zone, a particularly troublesome guerrilla stronghold straddling the main River channel to Saigon. This ship had formerly served with the French as the Arquebuse and was formerly a USN Landing Craft Support (LCS). (US Navy via Cressman)

(Above) A CCB moves along a river during operations against guerrilla forces south of Saigon. Note how the vessel has been heavily camouflaged in an attempt to break up its outline. A US advisor can be seen standing amid ship with the captain of the CCB. (US Navy via Cressman)

(Above) Camouflaged RAG boats and their crews await the return of ARVN troops from a sweep ashore. Atempts to conceal riverine boats with paint or at least to break up their outline proved to be relatively ineffective and by the mid-1960s camouflage had almost ceased. (US Navy)

(Right) River Patrol Craft (RPC) were designed to replace some of the older French boats used by the Vietnamese. A few RPCs were used by the US for minesweeping but the majority served with the Vietnamese Navy. The RPC carried both .30 and .50 caliber machineguns. (US Army)

(Below) Often times the only means of getting men and supplies to sites in the Mekong Delta was by water. This LCM has just arrived at the isolated outpost of Ly Van Manh with a load of construction materials. (US Army)

(Above) Attempts were made to modernize the Junk Force in the mid-1960s. Newer, motorized junks were acquired to replace the old unpowered Junks which were either discarded or motorized. The force was eventually absorbed into the regular Navy which helped improve morale, pay, and training. (US Navy)

(Below) The Nguyen Ngoc Long (HQ-230) on the Go Cong river. Though these LSSLs carried a fairly heavy complement of armament, their high profile made them easy targets for Viet Cong gunners on shore; a number of the LSSLs suffered severe damage when caught in ambushes. But while the high silhouette of the bridge provided a tempting target it also gave the crew a good vantage point from which to direct fire on the guerrillas. (US Navy)

THE UNITED STATES BROWN WATER NAVY

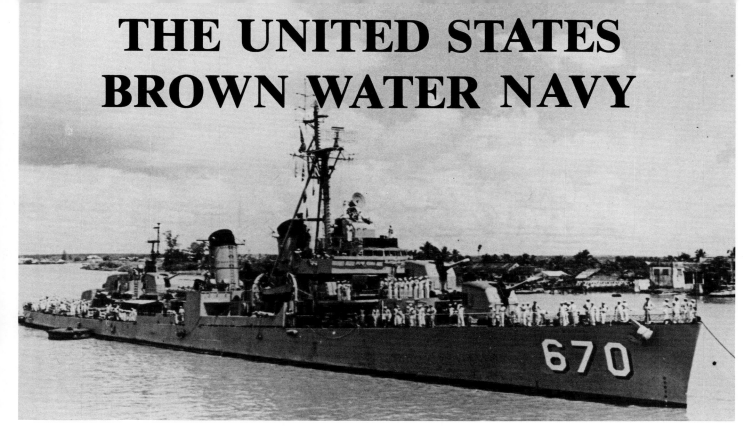

COASTAL FORCES

Market Time (Task Force 115)

The first large scale operational participation of the US Navy in the Vietnam War came about due to an action known as the *Vung Ro Incident*. On 16 February 1965, a US Army helicopter spotted a heavily camouflaged trawler laying in Vung Ro Bay north of Nha Trang. Air strikes were called in on the anchored ship and stacks of supplies on the beach. After the trawler settled in the shallow water plans were made to send ARVN troops aboard navy ships to check out the area. However, due to conflicting orders and Vietnamese ineptness little was done to secure the area for two days. During the interim the *VC* was able to salvage most of the weapons, ammunition, and medical supplies still aboard the trawler, and when ARVN forces finally took the area little was left, much to the disgust of their American advisors.

Due to the now blatant seaborne infiltration by the *VC*, and the dismal performance of Vietnamese forces, General Westmoreland requested a meeting with top level US Navy commanders to discuss the incident. Held on 3 March, the joint conference, after investigating the action, recommended that the US Navy take a direct role in interdicting seaborne infiltration, both as a means of stopping it, and inspiring the Vietnamese to do a more creditable job.

This recommendation won almost immediate approval from the Joint Chiefs of Staff and on 16 March two destroyers, the Higbee (DD 806) and Black (DD 666) began patrolling off the coast. The destroyers were joined by Navy P-2V Neptunes from Tan Son Nhut airbase which had begun aerial surveillance shortly after the March meeting. A week later, on 24 March, the operation received the code name MARKET PLACE.

Within a short time the sea and air forces engaged in MARKET PLACE had increased substantially. By the beginning of April twenty-eight ships, under the control of Task Force 71 (TF 71) were operating off the Vietnamese coast. To counter infiltration close inshore, fast patrol craft (PCFs), called 'Swifts', were introduced to carry out close in-shore patrol work. To further supplement these new assets the US Coast Guard was ordered to deploy Squadron One, composed of seventeen 82 foot cutters (WPBs), for service with TF 71.

By late spring, it was decided in Washington to transfer control of TF 71 to the US Naval Command in Saigon. In August this was formalized when operational control of the force passed from the Pacific Fleet to General Westmoreland. At the same time the commander of TF 71 relinquished his control of the task force, it was redesignated to Task Force 115 (TF 115) under the code name Market Time.

One of the first shows of United States support for the newly constituted Republic of Vietnam was a visit by an American destroyer squadron in October of 1953. The Fletcher class destroyer, USS Dortch (DD-670), sailed up the river to Saigon for a two day visit. (US Navy)

During this period, the first significant contact between the US Navy and *VC*, since the *Vung Ro Incident*, took place when the USS Buck (DD 761) spotted a junk that was acting strangely. The destroyer stopped the vessel and upon boarding found arms and supplies aboard. The crew was taken into custody and they, along with the material, were turned over to the South Vietnamese. However, despite this successful encounter the forces available to Market Time were stretched thin, especially for in-shore work. This was brought to the attention of Defense Secretary McNamara during one of his fact finding missions to Vietnam. As a result, the number of Swift boats was increased from thirty-six to fifty-four, and were divided equally betweeen bases at Vung Tau, Qui Nhon, and Cam Ranh Bay.

To regulate the activities generated by the sudden influx of American forces, TF 115 set up nine coastal patrol areas. Each station was roughly thirty to forty miles in width and eighty to one hundred twenty miles long. Each had either a destroyer escort (DE) or minesweeper (MSO) assigned to it. At either end of the coast of Vietnam, Coast Guard cutters from Squadron One set up barrier patrols. As operations continued through the summer and fall of 1965, naval authorities, in September, reviewed the overall situation and structure of Market Time forces. As a result of this review, a number of

As the United States became more deeply involved in the Vietnam conflict additional advisors were sent to work with Vietnamese Naval units. These American Navy officers wait aboard a command junk prior to an operation by Vietnamese forces. The Vietnamese crewman near the bow is wearing a French helmet. A USN LST can be seen moored in the background. (US Navy)

The enemy also tried to move material by ocean going vessels, such as this trawler. It was the botched handling by the Vietnamese Navy of the interception of an enemy trawler at Vung Ro Bay that resulted in the deployment of US Naval forces on a substantial basis into Vietnamese waters. (US Navy)

US advisors worked with the Vietnamese Navy in all facets of naval operations. This advisor, Lieutenant (JG) Jim Fought, armed with an M-14 rifle, served with a junk unit along the coast to counter communist infiltration from the sea. Air recognition markings are painted on the deck so that US or VNAF aircraft would not attack the junk by mistake. (US Navy)

The Viet Cong were supplied from the sea by a variety of craft. Small coastal junks, such as this one, were often used to move arms and supplies from communist enclaves along the northern coast to areas further south. Because of the large number of boats plying the coast, surveillance was a serious problem. (US Navy)

(Above) For close-in work Patrol Craft, Coastal (Fast) (PCFs), nicknamed 'Swift boats', with their shallow draft were ideal. These boats, modified from crew boats used to serve commercial oil rigs, carried a twin machine gun turret atop the cabin and mortar/machine gun combination aft. (US Navy)

(Below) Market Time, as the coastal forces of the 'brown water navy' was code named, was composed of a number of different units. Destroyers (DDs), destroyer escorts (DEs), and minesweepers (MSOs) such as USS Pledge (MSO-492) seen here, patrolled the ocean out to forty miles from the Vietnamese coast. (US Navy)

(Above) Closer to the shore the Coast Guard kept an eye for small vessels which operated in the shallower coastal regions. The USCG cutter Point Young (CG 82303) is patrolling a few miles off the coast on a clear day. At night or in inclement weather the cutters used radar to spot suspicious traffic. These cutters were armed with four .50 caliber machine guns in single mounts on the stern and a combination mortar/.50 caliber machine gun in the bow. (US Coast Guard via Cressman)

recommendations were made to increase TF 115's effectiveness. These recommendations included an increase of off-shore patrol ships from nine to fourteen and the addition of another radar equipped LST to supplement the three already operating in the Mekong Delta. The number of small craft was also felt to be understrength. This led to an increase in 'Swift' boats to eighty-four and the WPBs to twenty-six.

The most significant recommendation made was to establish a *river patrol force* to operate along the major rivers in specially equipped LSTs. This force was not to be part of TF 115 but rather a separate unit since its function, responsibility, and employment would be quite different from Market Time forces. This decision would open up a totally new area of operations to naval forces, and bring US sailors virtually into hand to hand combat with communist troops.

P5M Marlin flying boats were used until their withdrawal from active duty in 1967. These seaplanes operated from tenders based at Cam RanhBay and Cong Son Island. This Marlin, from VP-48, is being lifted out of the water by the tender Pine Island for maintenance. The symbols just behind the trailing edge of the wing represent eighteen ships sighted by the aircraft during its numerous patrols. Just under the cockpit is the aircraft's name, 'Road Runner', and a drawing of the popular cartoon character. (US Navy)

(Below) Aerial surveillance was provided by Navy patrol squadrons operating a number of different aircraft types. This SP-2H Neptune checks out a junk south of Vung Tau, reporting its position to Market Time surface craft. The aircraft is from VP-1 and initially operated out of Tan Son Nhut airfield north of Saigon. (US Navy/Naval Aviation History via Grossnick)

Aerial Surveillance

Additional Market Time surface vessels increased its surveillance capabilities but there was still not enough ships to adequately patrol the large expanse of ocean off the Vietnamese coast. The Navy therefore decided to increase the number of aircraft available to the commander of TF 115 for patrol work. Additional P-2V Neptunes began flying out of Tan Son Nhut to supplement the original Neptune force which had begun patrolling earlier that spring. These Neptunes were given responsibility for the area from Vung Tau south to An Thoi, which included the vital Mekong Delta and the major rivers which dissected this important population and agricultural area. Aiding the P-2V Neptunes were P-5 Marlins, the last operational flying boat in the US Navy inventory. The Marlins, supported by seaplane tenders at Cam Rahn Bay and Con Son Island, flew daily missions over the numerous rivers and canals of the delta region until 1967. By then, there were enough land based patrol aircraft available to allow the Navy to phase out the Marlins which were not as capable and were more costly to operate than their landbased counterparts.

The job of patrolling the area from Vung Tau north to the DMZ was the responsibility of P-3 Orions based at Sangley Point in the Phillippines. With more sophisticated radar, the Orions were ideal for covering this broad expanse of ocean. The P-3's range and better crew facilities also allowed it to stay on station longer and cut down on the possibility of the *VC* slipping ships through the area during transit time. As the war progressed P-3s expanded their operations and replaced the Marlins. They also began rotating out of Cam Rah Bay where they were joined by additional Neptunes. Late in the war Neptunes were also phased out with P-3s Orions taking over all Navy patrol responsibilities.

These P-3s from VP-50 sit at the airfield near Cam Ranh Bay surrounded by barbed wire and armed guards against communist sabotage. Normally Orions operated out of the Philippines while Neptunes flew from bases in Vietnam. (US Navy/Naval Aviation History via Grossnick)

Harbor Defense

While Market Time's primary responsibility was to patrol the coastal waters and cut off enemy supplies it also had the responsibility for harbor defense at the five main ports of South Vietnam. In 1964 *Viet Cong* swimmers had attached explosives to a US aircraft transport in Saigon and sank the ship at her berth. Realizing the need to protect ships against such attacks the Navy came up with the concept of South East Asia Semi-Permanent Harbor Protection (SEASHARP) to counter this new enemy threat.

After a period of trial and error SEASHARP evolved into a formalized security structure made up of three components. At each harbor a site was selected for a base of operations and maintenance facility. This base of operations facility housed the personnel needed to provide logistics and support for the patrol units. In addition this site also contained the Harbor Entrance Central Post (HECP) which functioned as a command post which was equipped with radios, radar, and a plot of all the ships in the harbor. From the HECP patrol boats were controlled and vectored to suspicious targets entering the harbor. The second component of SEASHAP was the Harbor Patrol Element (HPE) made up of patrol boats and their crews who kept the harbor under constant patrol and monitored the vast array of small craft which plied the harbors. These HPE boats normally carried their own radar and were armed with machine guns and a variety of small arms for use by the crew. A wide variety of boat types were employed by the HPE including Boston Whalers and picket boats but the backbone of the HPE was the LCPL Mark XI, a thirty-six foot long utility boat. The final component of each SEASHARP unit was an Explosive Ordnance Disposal (EOD) team which was responsible for making inspections of ship hulls and anchorage sites.

As the concept of harbor defense evolved, SEASHARP was redesignated the Inshore Undersea War Group (IUWG), with each unit being given a designation from one to five. The parent organization was Mine Force Pacific Fleet, even though they functioned under TF 115. During the period in which the IUWG was training and being deployed the task of harbor defense fell upon Mobile Inshore Undersea War Surveillance (MIUWS) teams which were sent TDY from their home ports in the United States. These units were capable of deploying on short notice for a limited time to ports in hostile areas. However, they lacked the capability of long term employment and were withdrawn when the IUWGs became operational.

With their creation in 1967, the IUWGs took over the bulk of harbor defenses in the five ports where they were stationed. However, harbor defense was separated from port security which was the responsibility of the Army. The division of these duties between the two services was arrived at by a very simple means. As long as a ship was tied up to a pier IUWG detachments were responsible for its security. Once the ship moored alongside a pier, the Army took over security. The only exception to this division of responsibility was at the port of Da Nang where the Navy carried out both tasks under the direction of Naval Support Activities (NSA) Da Nang.

The IUWGs were responsible for the defense of their respective harbors. The Harbor Entrance Central Post kept a close watch on the overall anchorage, and the small patrol craft of the HPE maintained visual contact over their individual patrol areas, their primary job being to deter attempts by VC swimmers and small craft to carry out sabotage missions. To do this HPE crews often spent as much as twelve hours on patrol checking out the multitude of civilian junks and trawlers which plied the harbors daily. To aid the HPE in their searches the Vietnamese Navy or National Police provided interpreters to assist the Americans. In a single day's patrol HPE crews might examine hundreds of small craft, and while this task proved monotonous sailors of the HPE still had to be constantly alert, because if the HPE failed to detect an infiltrating group of saboteurs, the enemy stood a good chance of inflicting severe damage to the moored ships.

The IUWGs remained in Vietnam until 1971 when they were pulled out as part of the American withdrawal program. The *Viet Cong* were never able to mount an effective sabotage campaign against the various anchorages under IUW protection. Some damage was done by the enemy, but it was of a minor nature and the *VC* never accomplished anything of significance. Upon their redeployment stateside, harbor defense was turned over to the Vietnamese Navy, but some IUW personnel remained behind to serve as advisors. With their help the Vietnamese were able to keep the harbors safe. When the final pullout of US troops occurred in 1972, and the Vietnamese took over harbor security completely they continued to keep the anchorages secure until the final collapse of the country some three years later.

United States Coast Guard

As in past wars the United States Coast Guard was called upon to supplement US Naval forces in the war zone. Due to the service's role in coastal patrol and rescue it had a number of craft that were specifically designed for in-shore work. Thus, in the early phases of Market Time the USCG boats bore much of the coastal patrol work until additional USN assets were able to take over the work load. The initial request for USCG assistance came in mid-April of 1965 when the Secretary of the Navy inquired about available assets from the Treasury Department, under which the Coast Guard operated during peacetime. After a series of interviews between the officials concerned, it was decided to deploy seventeen 82 foot patrol boat (WPBs) for inshore work along the coast of Vietnam. By the end of May the boats had been loaded aboard cargo ships and were on their way to Subic Bay in the Philippines which was to serve as an advanced training facility to ready the crews for deployment to the war zone. Personnel of the first unit, Coast Guard Squadron One (RONONE), was commissioned on 27 May 1965 at the Coast Guard base at Alemeda, California, receiving an intense course in survival training following commissioning, along with instruction on weapons systems, patrol procedures, combat indoctrination, and a variety of other subjects in preparation for their service in Vietnam. Upon completion of this training the officers and men followed their WPBs to Subic Bay where they took part in refresher training and put their cutters through shakedown cruises.

By mid-July, the first of the squadron's two sub-units, Division Twelve,

In the mid-1960s a new type of ship was sent to Vietnam to aid Market Time forces. This fast new motor gunboat (updated to patrol gunboat in 1967) gave the navy the ability to bring a relatively heavy fire to bear on in-shore patrols from a ship of fairly shallow draft. USS Gallup (PG-85) moves at high speed through the coastal waters off Vietnam. It is claimed that this class of ship was able to go from 0 to 40 knots in sixty seconds. (US Navy)

was operational and on 15 July it departed Subic Bay for Da Nang near the DMZ. Division Eleven was ready by 20 July and set sail for An Thoi in the Gulf of Thailand. At month's end, Task Force 115 (Market Time) was officially established and RONONE became part of the organization. To coordinate the numerous units which comprised TF 115, five Coastal Surveillance Centers (CSCs) were set up at Da Dang, Qui Nhon, Nha Trang, Vung Tau, and An Thoi. Working with these centers RONONE cutters were assigned to different patrol stations off the northern and southern ends of Vietnam. At these stations the cutters came under the direction of the minesweeper or destroyer escort that maintained the outer barrier patrol, and which provided the Coast Guard cutters with radar and navigational aids. In turn the USCG cutters provided similar aid to US and Vietnamese units on in-shore patrol, and, if the need arose, also provided fire support.

During this early period USCG cutters intercepted numerous junks and sampans carrying enemy soldiers and/or supplies. Sometimes resistance occurred but the cutter's .50 caliber machine guns and mortars were more than a match for the small arms fire they encountered. In addition to these firefights the WPBs were called upon on several occasions to provide support for US Special Forces and ARVN units along the coast. During these engagements the indirect fire of the 81mm mortar on the bow of these cutters proved to be especially effective in providing fire support and illumination at night.

While the two Coast Guard divisions were doing a good job in their respective sectors, the whole central coast of South Vietnam was uncovered. To alleviate this problem nine additional Coast Guard cutters were reassigned from other duties to form a third division to cover the vital center area. Division Thirteen was officially formed on 12 December 1965, and ready for duty in early February of 1966. It left Subic Bay on 12 February for Vung Tau and by the end of the month its cutters were on station alongside other Market Time forces.

Throughout the spring all three division had numerous run-ins with small junks carrying contraband, and carried out the occasional fire support mission for troops ashore. In May the action heated up. The cutter Point Grey (WPB 82324) came across a 120 foot trawler near the Cau Mau peninsula which acted very suspicious. When the cutter moved in to investigate, the trawler, in an effort to escape, beached itself. The Grey tried to put a boarding party on the ship, but intense automatic fire from the beach forced the cutter away. Calling for back-up, the Grey was joined by the Point Cypress

(WPB 82326) and sank the trawler in shallow water. Navy divers later salvaged a huge amount of weapons and ammunition.

A month later, on 20 June, a 98 foot trawler was spotted by the Point League (WPB 82304) near Vung Tau. As the cutter approached, she came under fire from the trawler. The Point League returned the fire forcing the trawler to turn shoreward in an attempt to escape. Hearing the cutter's call for assistance, the Point Slocum (WPB 82313) and Point Hudson (WPB 82322) soon arrived, by which time the trawler had been forced aground. After being boarded, the ship was refloated and towed back to Vung Tau where several tons of arms, ammunition, and medical supplies were uncovered in her holds.

The rest of the summer saw little action with the enemy but a case of mistaken identity resulted in a tragic incident. During routine night patrol near the DMZ in August the Point Welcome (WPB 82329) was illuminated by friendly aircraft. Despite attempts to identify herself, the cutter was attacked by the aircraft and received a number of hits. Burning, the cutter was beached and the crew abandoned her in the face of continuing attacks. When the action was finally over, two Coast Guardsmen were dead and three were wounded. The Point Welcome, severely damaged, was eventually refloated and towed to Da Nang for repairs.

During the remainder of 1966 and the early part of 1967 no significant action occurred with communist trawlers. The three divisions continued to intercept small coastal junks, and, in addition, rescued a number of downed aircrews and Vietnamese sailors from the South China Sea. In March, a 120 foot trawler attempted to run the patrol barrier near the DMZ. Various Market Time forces, including the Point Ellis (WPB 82330) shadowed the vessel until it neared the coast. Realizing that they were trapped, the crew ran the trawler aground after a short firefight. The enemy crew was able to destroy some of the cargo, but a large part of it was subsequently recovered after the vessel was towed to Da Nang.

This shadowing and interception brought to light the serious shortage of forces which still faced TF 115. A large number of surface units had been involved in the operation and as a result, some sectors were left unguarded during the chase. Early in 1967, the Navy had requested the Coast Guard to provide five high endurance cutters (WHECs) to supplement Market Time units. With the March interception still fresh in their memories, Coast Guard officials organized Squadron Three (RONTHREE) at Pearl Harbor on 24 April 1967. It left Pearl two days later and arrived at Subic Bay on 10 May. By month's end the five cutters were on station with TF 115 which assigned them, because of their shallow draft, to the Gulf of Thailand. There, the squadron worked the outer barrier patrol and provided fire support with their five inch guns. They also served as logistic bases for the WPBs and Swift boats of the in-shore patrol force. Often the WHECs carried a replacement crew for the Swifts so that the small craft could stay on station for extended periods of time. In turn the Coast Guard cutters were usually resupplied by the oilers, ammunition, and supply ships of the 7th Fleet. This allowed the cutters to stay on station for long periods of time, docking only when repairs were necessary or to give their crews a short break from sea duty.

Throughout the remainder of the summer of 1967 few major contacts occurred. The most significant came in July when the Point Orient (WPB 82319) ran a 120 foot trawler aground and captured a large amount of weapons. However, a major change in operational procedure occurred early in the fall when TF 115 decided to take advantage of the ocean going

An enemy hundred foot trawler has been run aground by the USCG Point League (CG 82304) near the village of Ba Dong. Note that each of the crewmen are wearing flak jackets as protection from enemy small arms fire. Market Garden forces working together, vectored enemy vessels before they reached safety and unload their cargo. (US Navy)

This steel hulled trawler, beached by its crew rather than suffer boarding, was later salvaged by the South Vietnamese who recovered over 250 tons of supplies and arms. (US Navy)

On patrol USS Ready (PG 87) is one of the new fast patrol gunboats designed for blockade and surveillance. However, its large size and shallow draft allowed longer patrols, heavier weapons and the ability to operate very close to the shore in order to provide support for US and ARVN troops along the shore. Besides the cannon armed forward turret and twin .50 caliber positions amidship, the superstructure bristles with machine gun mounts. (US Navy)

capabilities of the WPBs and have them alternate their patrol stations with the PCFs. This alternation was based on weather conditions, which allowed the 'Swift' boats to operate far more effectively since they could not function in heavy weather. Though not a popular change with Coast Guard personnel, it was accepted as just one more duty they had to perform.

The beginning of 1968 saw the largest battle of the entire war for the barrier patrol when North Vietnam made a desperate attempt to infiltrate men and supplies during the end of February to bolster their failing Tet offensive. Near Da Nang the cutter Androscoggin (WHEC 68), along with the Point Grey (WPB 82324), Point Welcome (WPB 82329) and a PCF spotted a trawler close inshore. After challenging the intruder, the force put the ship under fire and drove it aground, where its crew destroyed it with explosives. Further south, near Nha Trang, another trawler was spotted by Naval and Coast Guard units which also forced her ashore. As these units closed in on the trawler, heavy defensive fire was encountered. Pulling back beyond range of this fire, the cutters opened up with 81mm mortars, scoring several hits which destroyed the vessel. A third trawler was encountered off the Cau Mau peninsula by the Winona (WHEC 65), Point Grace (WPB 82323), Point Marone (WPB 82331), Point Hudson (WPB 82322) and Swift boats. Taking heavy fire, the trawler exploded and disappeared from the radar scope. Another trawler, spotted by the Minnetonka (WHEC 67) just beyond Vietnamese waters, decided to play it safe and fled back to safety. During the course of just one evening, three trawlers were destroyed in the biggest single engagement of the war by Market Time forces.

This battle was the high point of the Coast Guard's effort in Vietnam. During the rest of 1968, only an occasional contact resulted during the numerous patrols carried out by the WPBs and WHECs. The larger cutters, with their heavier armament, participated in a number of fire support missions for US Army and ARVN troops, particularly in the Cau Mau peninsula area. These missions provided the only instances where the large cutters actually encountered the enemy. Rarely during their daily patrol operations were any of the small craft found to be carrying weapons or supplies. Following their heavy losses in February, North Vietnam opted not to try to run trawlers through the barrier patrols. The Coast Guard crews settled into an almost peacetime routine, occasionally rescuing downed aviators and fishermen in trouble, or providing emergency medical aid for allied personnel when the need arose. Some of the cutters carried out hydrographic surveys of uncharted areas but on the whole the remainder of 1968 was a quiet year.

The year 1969 saw a number of changes for Coast Guard forces engaged in Vietnam. US authorities decided to turn over a greater share of the war to the Vietnamese, and as part of this program the Coast Guard was instructed to begin training Vietnamese sailors so that eventually they could take over the 82 foot cutters of all three divisions. This transition began in January and by the spring of 1969 the training program was well enough along to transfer the Point Garnet (WPB 82310) and the Point League (WPB 82304) over to the Vietnamese. During this period, the first of a new class of cutter, the Hamilton (WHEC 715), arrived off the coast to relieve the older cutters which dated back to World War Two. With more modern armament, radar, and flight facilities, these new arrivals soon showed how superior they were to the older vessels.

One result of these new additions was the decision to transfer a number of the older cutters to the South Vietnamese Navy to give it more depth for offshore patrolling. In early 1970, two more cutters, the Bering Strait (WHEC 382) and Yakutat (WHEC 380) were selected for transfer to the Vietnamese.

Eventually two more cutters, the Castle Rock (WHEC 383) and Cook Inlet (WHEC 384) were also transferred to the Vietnamese Navy. The turnover of Coast Guard assets to the Vietnamese continued throughout 1970, with the last of the 82 foot cutters being officially transferred by 15 August 1970. This also marked the formal disestablishment of Coast Guard Squadron One as a part of US forces in Vietnam. The larger cutters, however, stayed on duty for a while longer and were involved in two more battles with trawlers. On 20 November 1970, the Rush (WHEC 723) and Sherman (WHEC 720) destroyed a trawler with gunfire after it failed to stop. The following spring, on 11 April 1971, the Rush, in company with the Morgenthau (WHEC 722) sank a trawler near the Cau Mau peninsula. However, these were the parting shots for Coast Guard operated cutters. By the winter of 1971, only one USCG ship, the Cook Inlet was still patrolling off Vietnam under Coast Guard control, albeit with a largely Vietnamese crew. It was officially turned over to the Vietnamese Navy on 21 December 1971. A short time later RONTHREE was officially dissolved, thus ending another chapter in the annals of the United States Coast Guard history. As in past wars, their performance had been outstanding, but it had not been without cost. Seven Coast Guardsmen lost their lives and an additional fifty-three were wounded. Over one thousand North Vietnamese and *Viet Cong* were killed or wounded in actions with Coast Guard units while over ten thousand were detained for questioning by South Vietnamese authorities. By their actions off the Vietnamese coast, the Coast Guard helped stop the flow of arms, men, and munitions into South Vietnam and undoubtedly saved the lives of countless thousands of allied soldiers and Vietnamese civilians. No matter what the conditions were, these men carried out their assignments. No more can be asked of a fighting man than that.

This Landing Craft Personnel (Large) MK II (LCPL MK II), based in Cat Lo, cruises in Vung Tau harbor, the entrance to the main shipping channel to Saigon. The sharksmouth on the bow is an unusual marking for a small Navy craft. The aft .50 caliber machine gun has not been fitted. (US Navy)

IUW-65, a harbor patrol boat, looking more like a pleasure boat than a Navy picket vessel, stops to investigate a small Vietnamese boat. The harbor patrol boat's large size allowed the HPE to carry out longer patrols and gave it the ability to carry heavier weapons such as the twin .50 caliber machine guns mounted amidship. The crew are armed with shotguns, M-16s, and side arms. (US Navy)

A section of 'Swift Boats' move out from their base at Cat Lo on a patrol in the Rung Sat area, a longtime communist stronghold which bordered the main river to Saigon. Eventually Swifts, PBRs, and Navy SEALs effectively eliminated the VC threat posed in this area. The lead Swift Boat mounts a combination mortar/.50 caliber machinegun on the aft deck while the second boat mounts only a mortar. (US Navy)

The combination mortar/machine gun was mounted on Swift boats and 82 foot Coast Guard cutters . Because of the way the weapons were sited it was not possible to fire both at the same time. The oversized helmet worn by the gunner contains communication gear which is connected to the bridge via the cord running across the deck, allowing the boat commander to direct the gun fire. (US Navy via Bell)

When action occurred all hell broke loose. This Swift Boat gunner is firing on VC positions in the tree line along the shore. Smoke from VC return fire can be seen in the tree line along the river. Each boat in the line will bring the enemy position under fire as it passes, thus keeping up sustained fire on the guerrillas until air support arrives. (US Navy)

Much of the coastal patrolled region looked like the terrain this P5M is flying over. Such terrain provided excellent cover for the guerrillas as they moved men and materials. It also provided the VC with excellent cover to set up ambush sites for the various patrol craft. (US Navy)

A Neptune lifts off from Cam Rahn Bay for a patrol along the coast of southern South Vietnam. At first Neptunes worked out of Tan Son Nhut but later staged out of the base at Cam Rahn Bay. These and the other patrol aircraft were an integral part of the brown water fleet. (US Navy/Naval Aviation History via Grossnick)

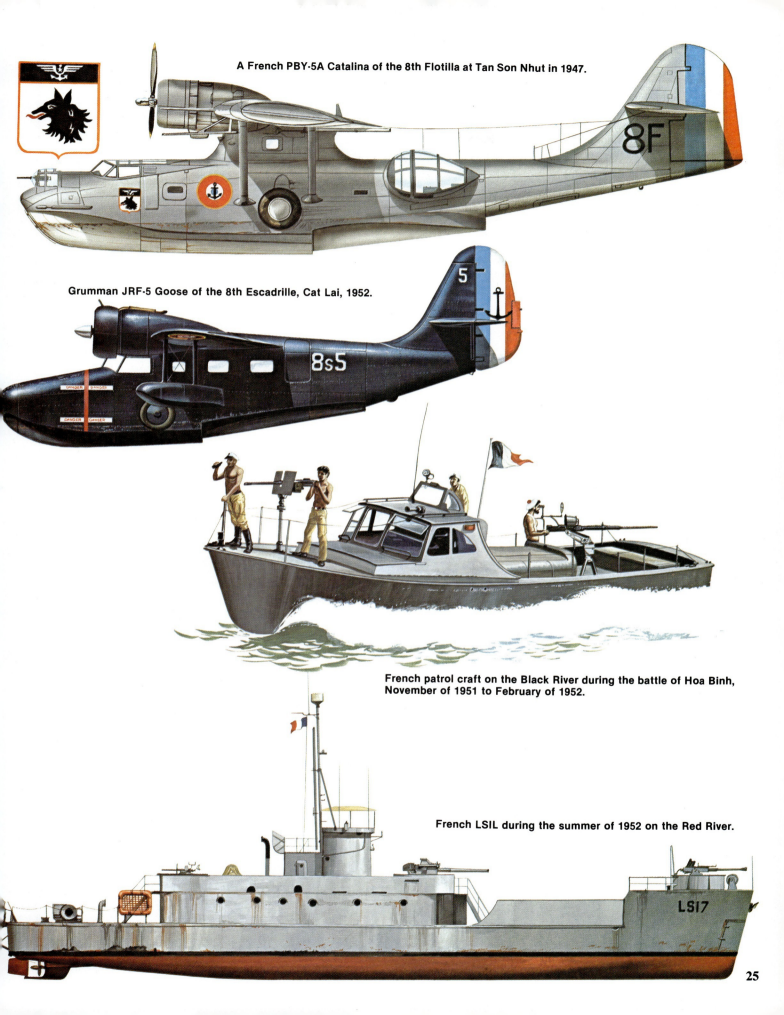

A French PBY-5A Catalina of the 8th Flotilla at Tan Son Nhut in 1947.

Grumman JRF-5 Goose of the 8th Escadrille, Cat Lai, 1952.

French patrol craft on the Black River during the battle of Hoa Binh, November of 1951 to February of 1952.

French LSIL during the summer of 1952 on the Red River.

Most patrols were long and tedious for the crews of the HPE boats. Rarely did much happen, yet these patrols were absolutely essential if the threat of enemy swimmers was to be kept in check. This LCPL has its guns covered for protection from salt spray and has its windshield lowered for a better view and increased air flow. (US Navy)

IUW 39, an LCPL from Unit 2 of IUW Group One, patrols in Cam Ranh Bay, which was the largest port in Vietnam and the main off loading point for much of the US supplies entering Vietnam. HPE crewmen spent long monotonous hours on patrol, with some patrols lasting up to fourteen hours. (US Navy)

Most of the day for harbor patrols meant search after search of countless Vietnamese small craft which plied the various ports. This Vietnamese junk is searched by US and Vietnamese personnel to see if it carries anything which does not match its manifest. (US Navy)

In addition to patrolling for infiltrators Market Time coastal units also supported landing operations along the coast. This Coast Guard cutter, the Point Kennedy (CG 82320), is taking part in OPERATION DECKHOUSE V, which involved a landing at the mouth of the Song Co Chien River. (US Navy)

For quick reaction to a threat the HPE could dispatch a 'Boston Whaler' manned by a two or three man detachment. These light skimmers, made of fiberglass, could hit speeds in excess of twenty knots which made them excellent craft for the HPE's quick reaction force. (US Navy)

As more of the new Asherville fast coastal gunboats were commissioned they were sent to Vietnam to aid the brown water coastal forces. The Tacoma (PG 92) and the Welch (PG 93) ply the waters of the South China Sea. Able to stay on station for long periods of time these craft were well liked by the crews for their living accommodations and stability while under way. (US Navy)

The Swifts were often pressed into duty as troop carriers. This PCF carries ARVN troops on a sweep of the Duong Keo river in the Ca Mau peninsula. One crewman mans a M-60 machine gun with a bi-pod on the bow. (US Navy)

At other times the Swifts carried EOD or SEAL teams on special missions. This boat has just returned from a mission with a demolition team which had an assignment on the upper reaches of the Cua Lon river. The rope ladder hanging on the bow was a commonly carried item to aid troops coming onto or leaving the boat. (US Navy)

With the need for additional ocean going ships to supplement existing Market Time assets, the Coast Guard was asked to provide additional ships. These five 311 foot High Endurance Cutters (WHECs) sit alongside the Navy repair ship USS Jason (AR-8) in Subic Bay. From left to right they are Half Moon, Yakutat, Gresham, Barataria, and Bering Strait. Bering Strait and Yakutat were later turned over to the South Vietnamese Navy. (USCG Via Cressman)

(Below) P3 Orions supplemented Neptunes and Marlins until the Marlins were retired and the Orions took over their duties. This Orion of VP-17 flies a reconnaissance over coastal marshland. (US Navy/Naval Aviation History via Grossnick)

(Above) The cutter Half Moon (W 378) takes on stores from the cargo ship USS Castor during patrol operations off the Ca Mau peninsula. Because of their ability to stay on station for long periods of time these cutters were used for sustained off-shore patrol. Unfortunately this allowed the crew little time ashore for recreation, but nevertheless morale aboard these ships never dropped. (USCG via Cressman)

Vietnamese River Assault Group (RAG) boat , Can Tho, 1966.

(Above Left) A Vietnamese motorized junk which replaced the earlier sail powered vessels of the Coastal Junk Force. The eye painted on the bow was for warding off evil spirits. The .30 caliber machine gun was used if the eye 'failed' to do the job. (US Navy)

(Right) A Vietnamese frogman prepares to enter the water for salvage work on the Co Chien River. The American advisor standing atop the RAG boat is Lieutenant Harold Meyerkord who was later killed in an ambush. For his courage during the ambush, Meryerkord was posthumously awarded the Navy Cross and later had a frigate named after him.

(Above) Another type of motorized junk with a more upswept bow also carries a protective eye on its bow, but instead of the standard .30 caliber machine gun on the bow a more potent .50 caliber machinegun has been mounted with a protective shield. (Chenoweth)

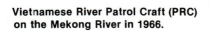

Vietnamese River Patrol Craft (PRC) on the Mekong River in 1966.

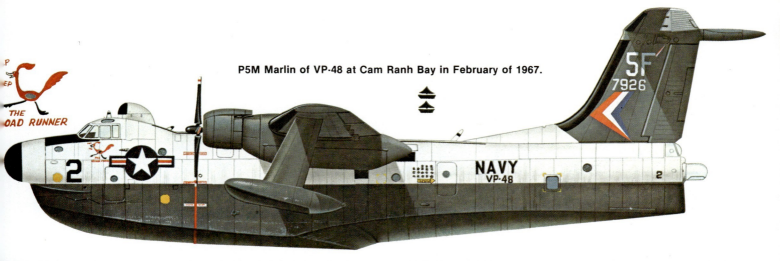

P5M Marlin of VP-48 at Cam Ranh Bay in February of 1967.

(Above Right) An SP-2H of VP-1 at Da Nang in 1967. During the early years of US participation in the war Neptunes formed the backbone of the landbased patrol force until replaced by the P-3 Orion. (Hansen via Mutza)

(Above) Supplementing the P-2 Neptunes were P5M Marlins which operated from seaplane tenders off the coast. A Marlin under going maintenance rests on the deck of a tender off Cam Rahn Bay. (US Navy)

(Right) These two AP-2H Neptune gunships sit in front of a row of Neptunes at Cam Ranh Bay in 1967. Note the jet engine silencers and FLIR/ILL TV chin additions to the two aircraft. (US Navy)

PCF MK I 'Swift Boat' during OPERATION GIANT SLINGSHOT in January of 1969.

RIVER FORCES
Game Warden (TF 116)

As a result of recommendations made by Naval authorities in September of 1965, a river patrol force, designated Task Force 116 and code named Game Warden, was formally established on 18 December 1965. This force was assigned the responsibility of helping Vietnamese river forces in denying the VC the use of the inland waterways. As originally envisioned the inland brown water force was to be composed of 120 specially designed River Patrol Boats (PBRs), twenty landing craft (LCVPs), a Landing Ship Drydock (LSD), a Landing Ship Tank (LST), and eight UH-1B Huey helicopters. This LSD and LST would serve as major support ships until the arrival of four specially modified LSTs.

In February of 1966, the first contingent of Game Warden sailors arrived in Vietnam and a month later received their first PBRs. TF 116 was divided into two sub-sections, the Delta River Patrol Group (TF 116.1) and the Rung Sat Patrol Group (TF 116.2). From the authorized strength of 120 PBRs, eighty boats were to be assigned to the Delta Group and forty to the Rung Sat Group, this distribution being based on the anticipated requirements of each area. The first few months after TF 116 arrived in Vietnam were spent getting ready for the massive influx of men and material slated for duty under Game Warden. And while the first few PBRs began patrolling in March, it took time for the full complement of boats and crews to reach Vietnam. These first PBRs worked from shore bases at Nha Be and Cat Lo until the arrival of the first off-shore support ship. A great deal of experience and knowledge was gained from these early missions and was immediately transmitted back to the Naval Inshore Operations Training Center in California to improve the river patrol training syllabus.

The first off-shore support ship, the USS Tortuga (LSD-26) was anchored in the South China Sea between the mouths of the Bassac and Co Chien Rivers, beginning operations in May of 1966. Attached to the Tortuga were ten PBRs, a detachment of two helicopters and two air cushioned vehicles (PACVs). Unfortunately, this initial deployment ran into unfavorable weather conditions and heavy seas and high winds restricted PBR activity almost half the time; these conditions continued throughout the fall. Eventually it was decided to drop the idea of operating PBRs from support vessels anchored off the coast; the ships were moved into the more sheltered waters of the rivers themselves. This decision was made only with great reluctance because of the fear that such a move would expose these big ships to mines, underwater saboteurs, and enemy fire from shore.

Shortly after the Tortuga deployed, it was followed by the Belle Grove (LSD-2), the Comstock (LSD-19), and the Floyd County (LST-762). Each of these ships were fitted with a helicopter deck and anchorage facilities for PBRs, and while they temporarily filled the need for a floating base, they were only a stop gap measure until the specially configured LSTs arrived. When initial plans for Game Warden were drawn up, LSTs specially configured for PBR bases had been an integral part of the program. Four ships, the Garrett County (LST-786) the Harnett County (LST-821), the Hunterdon County (LST-838) and the Jennings County(LST-846) were pulled out of reserve and specially modified as floating PBR Bases. Each had a helicopter landing pad with lights for use during day or night, four additional boat

A PBR cuts through the waters of Kein Tuong province in search of guerrillas. While these small craft were capable of speeds up to twenty-five knots, they rarely operated at this speed unless under fire, or coming and going from a patrol assignment. (US Navy)

booms, a PBR machine shop in the tank well, as well as updated radio, navigational, and electronic equipment. The first of these converted LSTs arrived in November of 1966, and within another few months the other three also arrived. Three were assigned to the Bassac, Co Chien, and Ham Luong Rivers while the fourth was kept in rotating reserve. During its reserve period each LST received a general maintenance and overhaul at a repair facility outside of Vietnam; usually in Japan, the Philippines or Singapore. Each LST usually remained on station for about six months before it was rotated out for maintenance.

Initially these LSTs proved invaluable since there were few facilities in-country that could handle PBR operations. With their special gear, the LSTs provided critical supply and maintenance facilities for the small river boats which were unavailable at shore installations. However, as adequate facilities became available ashore, the limitations of the LSTs became increasingly obvious. During modification these LSTs had had everything conceivable stuffed into their hulls and were seriously over crowded. Facilities were limited, and even though a PBR unit could operate from each one, crowding in berthing, supply, maintenance, repair and crew quarters was a constant problem. However, the ships did fill a critical need when they first arrived in the fall of 1966 and provided a mobile platform which could be moved as required to areas where PBR operations were needed.

This mobility even allowed the LSTs to occasionally participate in the fire support role or engage targets of opportunity with their 40mm defensive guns. During the post-Tet attacks in May of 1968, the Jennings County was credited with seventeen VC killed during a fire support mission. While such actions showed that the LSTs could be used offensively, the initial fears of operating the big ships in confined conditions were still a big concern. This was brought home in December of 1968, when the Hunterdon County (LST 838) ran afoul of a VC ambush. She was hit by well sighted rocket and recoilless rifle fire from shore and suffered extensive structural damage. Two crewmen were killed and twenty-five wounded. This action had a sobering affect on sailors who tended to underrate the threat posed by the guerrillas to the large ships and helped impress on all personnel the need to be constantly on the alert.

River Patrol Boats (PBRs)

No boat came to symbolize the brown water navy like the PBRs which were the mainstay of river operations. These tiny craft were the spiritual descendants of the PT boats of World War Two.

When the Navy decided to commit river patrol forces to in-shore operations in Vietnam it found itself in need of a small fast patrol craft. Because of the time factor, the Navy was unable to formulate a new design and opted instead to seek a commercially available hull and modify it for use in the combat zone. What the Navy wanted was a small light boat with high speed, shallow draft, powered by a water-jet propulsion system. Numerous companies submitted their hulls for consideration and from these the Navy chose a fiberglass 'Hatteros' hull for production. A contract for 120 PBRs was

To support the PBRs four LSTs were pulled out of reserve and modified to support a detachment of PBRs and a helicopter element of HAL-3. Until fixed bases could be constructed in the delta these ships played a vital role in Game Warden operations. Seen here is the USS Harnett County (LST-821). (US Navy)

awarded in November of 1965 to United Boatbuilders of Belingham, Washington, for delivery by April 1966, at a unit cost of $75,000.

The end result of this was the Mark I Power Boat, River (PBR); a thirty-one foot long craft capable of speeds over 28 knots. It was powered by a General Motors 220hp diesel truck engine which provided 2800 RPMs direct drive for a Jacuzzi water jet propulsion pump. The boat's armament consisted of a twin .50 caliber machine gun turret in the bow, a single .50 caliber machine gun in the stern, and a M-60 machine gun and a Mark 18 40mm grenade launcher mounted amidship. In addition to this armament the crew also had their small arms. As the war progressed, a variety of weapons were fitted to the PBRs, including 90mm recoilless rifles, 60mm mortars, flamethrowers, and 20mm cannons. Despite all this armament the PBR drew only two feet of water and was extremely maneuverable since changing course only required a change in the direction of the water jet nozzle. For patrol work at night a Raytheon 1900/W radar unit was carried which allowed the crew to pick out small craft that were extremely difficult to spot in the inky darkness which enveloped the waterways after sundown.

After the initial run of PBR Mk Is, the PBR Mark II was introduced. Slightly larger with more powerful engines, the only significant difference between the Mk I and Mk II was the addition of aluminum gunwales on the Mk II to protect the hull from being torn up when coming along side sampans and junks.

Normally the PBR was manned by a four man crew — a first class petty officer, a gunner's mate, an engineman, and a seaman. The petty officer was the boat captain, the gunner's mate operated the forward fifties, the engineman was responsible for the powerplant, and usually he and the seaman manned the other weapons during a patrol. Each man was cross trained in the other jobs and could take over in case one of the other crewmen was wounded. Generally PBRs operated in a two boat section, and in addition to the regular crew one boat carried a patrol officer who was in charge of the operation. If a Vietnamese translator or policeman was carried he rode on the other boat.

While PBR patrols were often seen as adventurous or glamorous, in reality they were just like any military operation — long, tedious, and boring days that were sometimes punctuated by minutes of sheer terror. When contact with the enemy was made, all hell usually broke loose for a few minutes, until the action ended. Then the boring routine began again. Normally, PBR crews patrolled around 80 hours a week, half of which was at night. Usually the boat operated at reduced speed and only went to full power when contact with the *VC* was made, or while proceeding to and from their patrol areas. Often the PBR crew cut their engines and achored or drifted with the current so as not to give away their position. This was a particularly effective tactic at night and on many occassions the *VC* were totally surprised when a pair of PBRs suddenly came to life spitting out a hail of fire. Most of the daylight hours were spent checking the endless junks and sampans that moved up and down the numerous rivers and canals dissecting the Mekong Delta. At sundown all normal water traffic quickly disappeared and any craft found on the

Normally the PBRs idled slowly along searching the various junks and sampans which plied the numerous canals and rivers of Vietnam. This PBR checks out a small sampan for weapons and supplies. The Viet Cong were masters at concealing such material in the smallest of craft and only by checking every vessel thoroughly could the flow of supplies be stopped. Though dull and monotonous, US brown water sailors carried out their mission efficiently, severely cutting back the movement of supplies to the VC. (US Navy via Cressman)

The PBR carried heavy fire power for such a small boat. The forward turret carried a pair of .50 caliber machine guns and a co-axially mounted searchlight. Late in the war a 20mm cannon was fitted in the turret, replacing one of the fifties and was fired alongside the remaining fifty.

31

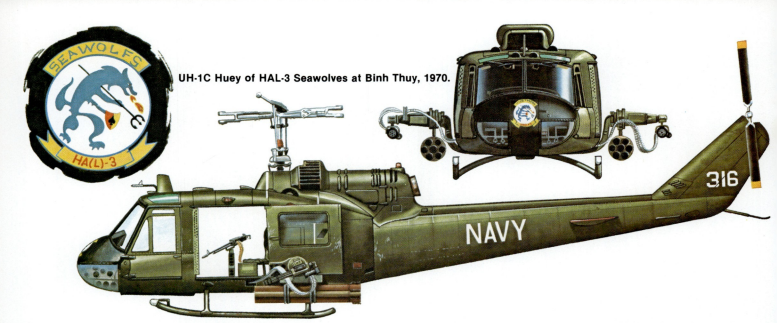

UH-1C Huey of HAL-3 Seawolves at Binh Thuy, 1970.

(Above) This UH-1M Huey of HAL-3 sits on the runway at Binh Thuy just prior to the squadron's stand down in January of 1972. The UH-1M was an upgraded version of the UH-1C. (Mesko)

(Above Right) A UH-1L Huey of the SEALORDS detachment at Binh Thuy in early 1971. The insignia on the nose is an old fashion admiral's hat with a black trident. Later in the war these overall Blue Hueys were used to supplement the strength of HAL-3. (Jacobs)

(Above) A group of US SEALs with their Vietnamese counterparts prior to a mission. The two men on the left are armed with models of the Stoner 63 A1 light machinegun while those in the middle carry various models of the M-16, and the man on the right has an M-60 fitted with an ammunition box. (US Navy via Simard)

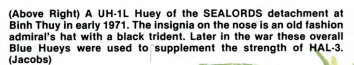

A SEAL, armed with Stoner 63 A1 MK 23 machinegun, in an ambush position on a path in the Mekong Delta.

Green over Gray OV-10A of VAL-4 Black Ponies at Vung Tau during the summer of 1969.

A Green over White OV-10 of VAL-4 at Binh Thuy in 1970/71. The unit's Broncos went through a number of marking changes during its short time in Vietnam. While mainly changes in nose numbers and location of squadron insignia, towards the end of the war the scheme of Green over White was changed on some aircraft to Light Gray over White. (US Navy via Michaels)

(Above Right and Right) Aside from the Black Pony artwork on the nose, VAL-4's OV-10s rarely carried paintings on their airframes. However, the ground crews, when time permitted, painted a variety of cartoons and slogans on ordnance and ordnance pods. Shown here are two such paintings, one on a gun pod and the other on a Zuni rocket launcher. The artist of both, Tom Fontana, is putting the finishing touches on the 'Roadrunner' with Testors paint. (Wiggs)

OV-10A of VAL-4 at Binh Thuy during 1972, in Gray scheme.

33

During a visit to Vietnam Secretary of the Navy, Paul R Ignatius, inspected the armament of a PBR. In the stern a variety of weapons could be mounted, in place of the usual fifty. This boat carries a rapid fire 40mm grenade launcher and a single M-60 machine gun on a starboard side mount behind the cockpit. An M-16 rifle and M-79 grenade launcher are carried as personal weapons by the crew. In addition, another .50 caliber machinegun is also mounted further aft. The crewmember demonstrating the grenade launcher is wearing the famed Black beret. (US Navy)

river after dark was considered to be the enemy and was immediately fired upon.

The communists did everything possible to avoid the PBRs, for, if *VC* junks or sampans were spotted by the PBRs, the enemy usually lost men and material. Stealth became the name of the game, as each side tried to outwit the other. The only time the guerrillas actively sought combat with the PBRs was when they wanted to divert attention away from another area or when they coveted a particular river crossing. These were usually well planned actions and the *VC* would set up defensive positions and site recoilless rifles, rocket propelled grenades (RPGs), and machine guns where they could do the most damage. Occasionally, the guerrillas tried to lure individual PBRs into small canals or tributaries and block their escape by dropping trees across the narrow watercourse. If a PBR could trapped it might be captured, providing the communists with a large amount of weapons and ammunition, not to mention the tremendous boost in morale it would give the guerrillas.

When PBRs encountered enemy junks or sampans the *VC* would usually try to make their escape up one of the numerous tributaries or canals which fed into the larger rivers. The communists knew that PBR crews were extremely wary of venturing up these narrow waterways where confined conditions severely restricted the PBRs maneuverability, giving the guerrillas a definite advantage should an ambush be sprung. Sometimes a PBR keeping up pursuit of an escaping enemy would stumble upon a concentration of enemy small craft. One such action occurred late on the afternoon of 31 October 1966. Two PBRs under the command of boatswain Mate First Class James Williams, came across two sampans which suddenly opened fire on them. Concentrated fire from the PBRs killed the crew of one sampan, but the other escaped up a nearby inlet. In pursuit, both boats began taking heavy fire from entrenched positions along the shore of the inlet. Pushing on through the fire from shore the PBRs came upon eight sampans and two junks. Fire was exchanged with the enemy boats, which were supported by automatic weapons fire from the shore. Williams, realizing that his pair of PBRs were up against a far larger force, maneuvered out of the killing zone and called for helicopter gunships. While doing this he discovered an even larger force of junks and sampans. Disregarding the odds Williams ordered an attack without waiting for the gunships to arrive. During the ensuing action the PBRs destroyed or damaged seven junks and fifty sampans. Low on ammunition, Williams nevertheless continued the attack when the helicopters arrived near dusk. To illuminate the remaining enemy forces he ordered the boats' searchlights turned on and pressed the attack. Finally, after nearly three hours of fighting, their ammunition almost exhausted, Williams ordered his PBRs to withdraw. Sixty-five enemy junks and sampans were destroyed during this action along with an undetermined number of guerrillas. For his courageous action during this patrol Williams was awarded the Congressional Medal of Honor.

PBR patrol tactics varied with the assignment but during a normal night patrol the boats usually operated with 400 to 600 yards distance between the *lead* boat and the *cover* boat. This allowed for the optimum use of radar and the optimum mutual protection. If one boat took fire from shore the other PBR could lend support and/or move to block the enemy's line of retreat. If a suspicious craft or movement on the shore caught their attention, one boat could move to investigate while the other kept its distance in case the *VC* were setting up an ambush. During the early days of the US river force it was standard procedure for PBRs to retire when engaged, and call for assistance. Unfortunately such tactics often allowed the guerrillas to escape. But following experiences gained during the 1968 TET offensive river force engagement procedures were changed when it was finally realized that a pair of PBRs could usually handle most situations. From then on the PBR crews had the option of continuing to engage the enemy rather than retreating and waiting for help.

PBR crews faced a wiley, and often fanatical enemy. When given the opportunity, the guerrillas would make the most of it, trying to inflict maximum damage and casualties on US forces. The brown water sailors had to be constantly alert for any signs of enemy activity during a patrol. On one such patrol, on 6 March 1967, Seaman David Ouellet, aboard PBR 124, spotted suspicious movement on the shore and alerted his boat captain. As the PBR made a highspeed run to investigate, an enemy grenade arched toward the engine compartment. Ouellet, the only crew member to see it coming, yelled a warning, and left his forward gun mount. Pushing the boat captain out of the way, Ouetllet covered the grenade with his own body a split second before it exploded, absorbing most of the blast himself. Critically wounded by the explosion, Ouellet was evacuated by helicopter to a hospital in Saigon where, despite every possible effort, he died on the operating table. In recognition of his conspicuous bravery, Ouellet was posthumously awarded the Congressional Medal of Honor on 30 January 1968. The medal was presented to his parents by Secretary of the Navy. Later a new navy frigate was named in his honor.

Game Warden Grows

Throughout 1967, TF 116 continued to expand from its modest beginnings. The original eighty PBRs in the Delta River Patrol Group were increased to 125 while the force in the Rung Sat stayed at about forty boats. New helicopter and support detachments were also added to the assets of the TF 116. An eventual strength level of 250 PBRs was approved by naval authorities, and with these increases came an expansion of the patrol areas, as well as deployment of PBRs to other corps areas. In September, ten boats were deployed to I Corps in OPERATION GREEN WAVE, as a test of the PBR's ability to operate in the rivers and lagoons of this area. And while not

Game Warden Operational Chain of Command (mid-1968)

COMUSMACV

COMNAVFORV

COMNAVSUPPACT DANANG	COMNAVSUPPACT SAIGON	CTF 115 (MARKET TIME)	CTF 116 (GAME WARDEN)	CTF 117 (MRF)	COM THIRD CONST. BRIGADE (SEABEES)
BASSAC RIVER PATROL GROUP	CO CHIEN RIVER PATROL GROUP	MY THO RIVER PATROL GROUP	RUNG SAT RIVER PATROL GROUP	UPPER DELTA RIVER PATROL GROUP	
PBR UNITS	PBR UNITS	PBR UNITS	PBR UNITS	PBR UNITS	
HELO UNITS	HELO UNITS	HELO UNITS	HELO UNITS	HELO UNITS	
SEAL UNIT	SEAL UNIT	SEAL UNIT	SEAL UNIT		
SEAL SUPPORT UNIT	SEAL SUPPORT UNIT	SEAL SUPPORT UNIT	SEAL SUPPORT UNIT		
LST UNIT	LST UNIT	LST UNIT	MINE COUNTER-MEASURES UNIT		

completely successful, the operation did give authorities in I Corps an idea of what the PBRs could do, which later resulted in requests for the assignment of Game Warden units in the I Corps area.

One problem which arose during PBR operations was their inability to operate in any kind of heavy seas. As originally planned Game Warden units were responsible for all aspects of river patrol. However, the PBRs took a tremendous beating from the rough waters at the mouths of the rivers, which not only hindered operations but often caused structural damage to the light boats. As a result, Com Nav For V* in Saigon changed the patrol boundaries in September of 1967. The demarcation line between Game Warden and Market Time was moved about five miles up river, allowing the PCFs, cutters, and gunboats of Market Time to work the mouths of the rivers, and at the same time allowed the PBRs of Game Warden to expand their patrols further up river.

As originally set up, TF 116 was composed of two PBR task groups, but the continued expansion of Game Warden assets in late 1967 resulted in the need for a change of this structure. In January 1968, the number of task groups was increased to four. The old Rung Sat Patrol Group remained unchanged, but the Delta River Patrol Group was split into three Groups, one each for the Bassac, Co Chien, and My Tho rivers. Each of the four groups had roughly the same assets though the Rung Sat Group received minesweepers in place of LSTs.

The expansion of Game Warden forces was interrupted in 1968 by the Tet offensive. Caught off guard by this surprise attack, many US and ARVN units were ill-prepared to react quickly to the fierce communist attack. Fortunately in the delta region, the PBRs were able to move swiftly to counter the VC's thrusts. Near the city of Chau Doc, PBRs surprised two Viet Cong battalions that were attacking the town, and causing heavy casualties, disrupted the VC attack. At Ben Tre, PBRs, supported by Seawolf Hueys, helped the city's defenders hold back the guerrillas for thirty-six hours, until a relief force arrived. Unfortunately, the communists were able to temporarily seize Vinh Long, but not before PBRs inflicted heavy casualties on them and evacuated most of the surviving allied personnel.

Once the initial impetus of the Tet Offensive was spent, Game Warden forces, along with the Mobile Riverine Force and other allied units, moved to reestablish control of the region. By the first week in April most of the lost ground had been retaken and conditions were basically back to the pre-Tet period. Cost to the PBR forces had been relatively light in comparison to other allied units. Eight sailors were killed, and 134 suffered some degree of wound. A large number of PBRs were damaged, but most were quickly repaired. Over 500 Viet Cong troops were confirmed killed during this period by Game Warden units. In addition, the guerrillas were unable to hold any major town for longer than a few days. As a result of their losses in the delta and elsewhere, VC activity dropped dramatically, and allied forces quickly reestablished and expanded areas under their control.

Following Tet, PBRs worked their way back into the familiar routine of monotonous patrolwork. In April a ten boat section was detached to Qui Nhon in II Corps for OPERATION MAENG HO II (FIERCE TIGER II).

Commander Naval Forces Vietnam.

(Below) PBRs could carry a variety of weapons used under special circumstances including 90mm recoilless rifles, mortars, and on one occasion a bow and arrow! This was used to fire flaming arrows into thatched huts to set them ablaze without exposing the crew to undue risks. However, the crew below finds that a flamethrower can do the job a whole lot better on this series of bunkers camouflaged as houses on a small tributary of the Bassac River southwest of Saigon. (Naval History Museum)

For a month this ten boat section supported Republic of Korean (ROK) troops whose area of responsibility included a number of waterways.

During the late spring of 1968 additional task group was formed in response to renewed guerrilla activity in the Delta. Designated the Upper Delta River Patrol Group, it was assigned to patrol the rivers near the Cambodian border and prevent the flow of NVA supplies from the 'sanctuaries' in Cambodia. At the same time, Game Warden units conducted patrols in the Saigon area to counter renewed enemy attacks against allied troops and installations.

This constant expansion of Game Warden activities resulted in increased contact with the VC who were trying to regain the initiative and recoup their losses after the Tet disaster. During a routine patrol PBR 750 cornered a sampan which it had pursued up a small canal off the My Tho river. As the PBR returned to the river, the VC unleashed a heavy barrage of rockets and automatic weapons fire on the patrol boat. Hit by two rockets, the craft began to burn furiously, and veered toward the beach out of control. Four more rockets slammed into the stricken PBR, causing more damage. One crewman, Gunner's Mate 2nd Class Patrick Ford, though seriously wounded, kept up a steady stream of fire on the guerrillas until flames drove him from his gun mount. With his clothes afire, and despite the intense pain of his own wounds Ford began pushing wounded crewmen over the side. Covered by fire from a second PBR, some of the men were rescued, but Ford was not among them. Within a short time additional PBRs, Vietnamese troops, and four helicopters from HAL-3 arrived in the area and began an extensive search for the missing crewmen. Two bodies were recovered, but no trace of Ford was found. With the approach of night search efforts were called off and the force retired from the area.

After the battle, a Viet Cong patrol found Ford's body washed up on the shoreline where it had been overlooked by the search forces. In a move which could only be expected from a cruel and vicious enemy, the VC staked out Ford's body in plain view on the river bank in hopes of enticing another PBR into an ambush. Fortunately, the local chief of a Popular Forces outpost learned of this and dispatched his troops to the scene where they routed the guerrillas and recovered the sailor's body. This action undoubtedly saved the PBRs from a deadly ambush if they had tried to recover the body on their

(Above) A PBR Mk II moves up a waterway in the Mekong Delta. The main visual difference between a Mk I and Mk II PBR was the curved portion of the superstructure on the Mk II. The round object atop the pole is a Raytheon 1900/W radar unit used for night patrols. (US Navy)

An Armored Troop Carrier (ATC) of River Assault Squadron 11, River Assault Division 112, in the Mekong Delta during the summer of 1967.

Younger readers may not remember 'IT'S A DAISY', but the generation which grew up during the 1950s and 1960s saw and heard it in advertisements for Daisy Air Rifles. These sailors pose in front of a turret with the potent armament of a .50 caliber machine gun with a .30 caliber gun mounted atop it. While such graffiti was often found on riverine vessels, official policy frowned on it. 'SAT CONG' roughly translates as 'KILL COMMUNISTS'. (Benedetti)

An Assault Support Patrol Boat (ASPB) moored along a shoreline during a break in operations. Note the use of heavy mesh screening around the forward turret to detonate RPGs before they hit the turret. (Benedetti)

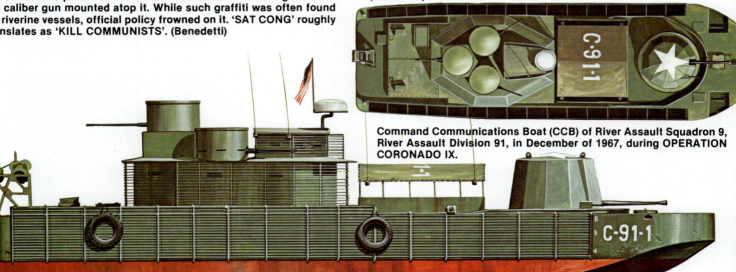

Command Communications Boat (CCB) of River Assault Squadron 9, River Assault Division 91, in December of 1967, during OPERATION CORONADO IX.

Assault Support Patrol Boat (ASPB) of River Assault Squadron 11, River Assault Division 111 during April of 1968 in the Giad Duc area.

Mines were a constant problem for the riverine forces. This Assault Support Patrol Boat (ASPB) shows just how deadly a mine could be. The mine detonated under the boat's stern, killing or seriously wounding the entire crew. (Beneditti)

A non-propelled barracks ship at Vung Tau. These barracks ships provided much needed berthing facilities for Mobile Riverine Force personnel but had to be towed from area to area which caused serious mobility problems for the force. (Mesko)

A UH-1H of the 336th Assault Helicopter Company landing on an ATC(H) of River Assault Division 91, June of 1968.

own. In recognition of his bravery, the navy posthumously awarded Ford the Navy Cross and later named a frigate (FFG 54) after him.

By late 1968, the enemy threat in most of the PBR patrolled areas had diminished to such a point that additional duties were assigned to the task groups. The most notable of these was OPERATION SEALORDS which began in the fall of 1968. Game Warden units teamed up with Market time 'Swift' boats and the Mobile Riverine Force to carry out a series of operations designed to interdict communist supplies from Cambodia. Market Time PCFs assumed responsibility for patrol areas further up river, freeing the PBRs to also move further up river.

At the same time SEALORDS was being carried out, steps were taken to provide Vietnamese naval personnel with training in PBR operations, with the eventual view of turning over patrol duties to them. This process of 'Vietnamizaion' was known in navy circles as the Accelerated Turnover Plan (ACTOV). It called for a sequential or gradual turnover of US assets to the Vietnamese, starting first with the combat forces and eventually following with the support units. In practice, a Vietnamese was assigned to a PBR where one of the US crewmen would train him in his job. When the Vietnamese sailor was fully trained, the American sailor would depart and another Vietnamese sailor would report for training by another US sailor. And while a few snags occasionally developed in the program, by early 1969 the phasing out of American manned PBRs was well under way, and by the fall of 1969 there were few boats operating with wholly American crews.

The last major operation in which the PBRs took part was during the spring of 1970, the invasion of Cambodia. Working with HAL-3 and VAL-4, the PBRs helped cover the advance into Cambodia of various US and Vietnamese riverine forces. Resistance was relatively light, and following the restrictions imposed by President Nixon, most of the combat was carried out by the Vietnamese. Following the Cambodian invasion, US naval strength was reduced dramatically. By the end of the summer US naval manpower had been cut in half and over eighty per cent of all operational craft had been turned over to the Vietnamese. The remaining US Naval personnel worked primarily in support, logistical, and advisory roles. In effect, this spelled the end of Game Warden. During the four years that Task Force 116 was in existence it had played a vital role in breaking the strangle hold which the *Viet Cong* had been holding on the the Mekong Delta. By aggressive patrolling, PBR sailors nearly stopped the flow of supplies and killed thousands of guerrillas. These patrols allowed the population of the delta to freely use the waterways without fear of attack by the communists and gave the South Vietnamese government the opportunity to extend its control over the region. At times the cost was high, but the PBR sailors never failed to carry out an

(Above) This PBR, with additional personnel aboard, cruises up the My Tho river during a sweep in the Mekong Delta. A PBR normally carried a crew of four or five depending on the mission. (US Navy)

(Above) Because of the constant wear and tear on them the PBRs needed periodic overhauls to keep them in service. This PBR is being lifted aboard the Garrett County (LST-786) to undergo maintenance and repair work. These support LSTs carried full equipment and spare parts to maintain the up to thirty PBRs which operated from the ships. (US Navy)

PBRs were used to carry both US and ARVN troops for amphibious landings against small enemy controlled islands along the waterways or working with Mobile Riverine Forces. This boat carries Vietnamese troops for an assault on Tan Dinh Island during OPERATION BOLD DRAGON III. (US Navy)

This landing craft has been converted to a river minesweeper (MSM) for use along the waterways in Vietnam. A number of these were employed along the river leading to Saigon and in I Corps. This particular vessel is coming into Nha Be after a mission on the Long Tau. (US Navy)

assignment. Through the efforts of men like Williams, Ouellet, and Ford, the Viet Cong were unable to impose their brand of barbarity on the Vietnamese delta population. Future events would undo what these men and countless thousands like them had accomplished, but these later events in no way diminish the outstanding job which these sailors did.

Task Force Clearwater

Until 1967 Game Warden forces operated almost exclusively in the Mekong Delta region. However, early in 1967, General Lewis Walt, the commander of US troops in I Corps, requested that MACV assign 30 to 40 PBRs or ASPBs to his command for use on the Perfume and Cua Viet Rivers which were vital supply routes in Thuo Thieu and Quang Tri provinces. The Perfume River served as the main line of transportation for men and materials coming up from the port of Da Nang to the old capital at Hue, and the Cua Viet River linked Dong Ha to the South China Sea. Each city was an important defensive and supply point for allied units in I Corps, and these narrow rivers provided a very tenuous link with the coastal ports; these rivers were weak points in the allied defensive strategy.

General Walt's concern over the situation was justified, but unfortunately, the Navy was not in a position to readily comply with his request. Neither TF 116 nor TF 117 were able to spare PBRs or ASPBs since both were in short supply already. However, recognizing that a real threat existed in I Corps, MACV worked out a temporary solution. Two mobile PBR support bases were ordered constructed for use on each river. The first, Mobile Support Base I (MB I), was constructed from Ammi barges and was ready to support ten boats by November of 1967. These ten boats were formed into River Division 55 and deployed to Da Nang in late November. Division 55 was followed shortly by River Section 521 onboard a Game Warden LST and MBI in early December. Upon arrival in Da Nang both units were sent to Tan My on the Perfume River and began conducting patrols in January of 1968.

Deployment of PBRs to the Perfume River quickly cleared up most of the VC threat in that area, but on the Cua Viet River a different solution was needed, and needed quickly. The Marine base at Khe Sanh had come under siege, and nearly all supplies for the Marine base passed through Dong Ha. Realizing the importance of the Cau Viet River the NVA and VC made a con-

certed effort using mines and carefully laid ambushes to choke of the flow of traffic up the river. When the enemy managed to sink an LST, MACV was finally forced to do something. Since Mobile Support Base II (MB II) was not yet ready, MACV ordered TF 117 to send River Assault Division 112 (RAD 112) less its ASPBs, to the Cua Viet. In part this decision was based on the fact that these riverine craft were more heavily armored than the PBRs and could better withstand an ambush. Another consideration was that if the NVA subjected the boats or their base to artillery fire it would be less effective against the armed river craft than against the lightly armored PBRs. However, the Tet Offensive slowed their deployment and it was not until March of 1968 that RAD 112 reached the Cua Viet.

The power of the Tet Offensive shocked US military officials and forced them to reevaluate existing policies. Attacks carried out against allied vessels on the Perfume and the Cua Viet Rivers during this period caused the new commander of I Corps, General Creighton Abrams, to request additional river craft and the organizing of a separate task force to protect and coordinate all river traffic in the region. In response Naval headquarters in Saigon set up Task Force Clearwater on 24 February aboard MB I*. Task Force Clearwater was divided into two task groups, the Hue River Security Group, and the Dong Ha River Security Group. The Hue Group included MB I, ten PBRs, and five LCM-6s converted for minesweeping duties, while the Dong Ha force had one CCB, three monitors, and ten ATCs.

With these forces, the Navy attempted to keep both waterways open. Supported by fixed wing aircraft, helicopters, artillery, and local ground troops, the PBRs and riverine craft patrolled the rivers countering attempts by the NVA and VC to close these vital supply lines. Despite their heroic efforts, the communists still managed to sink both logistical and escort craft, although neither river was ever closed. This renewed enemy effort prompted I Corps to request more PBRs since their speed allowed them to react more quickly to attacks than the slower moving riverine craft of the Dong Ha group. Ten more PBRs were deployed from forces in the Rung Sat. These arrived in two increments, five boats in May and five boats in June. They relieved RAD 112, which returned to the delta, although six ATCs were temporarily left behind for minesweeping work until five LCM-6s could be reconfigured for the minesweeping role. Later that summer three PACVs were reassigned from the delta to work with the Hue task group, and eight LCPLs, especially fitted for night surveillance work, augmented the PBRs of the Dong Ha section. These night surveillance LCPLs were fitted with a twenty-four inch zenon gas infrared searchlight and manned by Marines from a searchlight battery. In addition they carried a .50 and .30 caliber machine gun fore and aft along with the various small arms of the crew. They patrolled the Cua Viet from dusk to dawn in an attempt to cut down on communist mining activity at night. Though lightly armed compared to the PBRs they could better handle the heavy searchlight gear, and if a serious firefight developed they could call in PBRs for support.

By the fall of 1968, efforts to clear the Perfume River had succeeded. Enemy forces had been driven out of the area and the threat to shipping had all but disappeared. As a result, the PBRs began working the adjacent waterways together with elements of the 101st Airborne Division (Airmobile) in an

No task force number was ever assigned to Task Force Clearwater.

Following a request for assistance to help keep the Perfume and Cua Viet Rivers open brown water PBR and MRF units were dispatched to I Corps in Northern Vietnam. The crew of this PBR check the identification papers of the Vietnamese aboard a small sampan on the Perfume river. The sailor near the bow is armed with a M-16 while the one astern carries a shotgun, both wear flak jackets for protection against small arms fire. (US Navy)

River Patrol Force TF-116

LCPL at Cat Lo in November of 1966.

U.S. NAVAL FORCES VIETNAM

NAVAL ADVISORY GROUP VIETNAM

Minesweeping Boat (non-magnetic) (MSB) of Detachment A, Mine Squadron 11. This boat was sunk in a VC ambush on 15 February 1967.

This sharkmouthed Patrol Air cushion Vehicle (PACV) presents a formidable appearance as it moves across a dry rice paddy in the Mekong Delta. With the ability to operate on both land and water, and able to move over low obstacles, the PACV was ideally suited for use in the Delta region. Despite the PACV's effectiveness its high cost prohibited widespread use with only three machines seeing service with the Navy in Vietnam. (US Navy)

(Above) Since no facilities were available for the PBRs deployed to I Corps Mobile Base One (MB 1) was constructed from 'Ammi' barges and used as a floating base. (US Navy)

(Below) On the Cua Viet River the Navy decided to deploy the more heavily armored riverine craft of River Assault Division 112. This Monitor moves slowly along the river while its crew carefully watches the shoreline for any sign of activity. (US Army)

(Above) Upon arrival on the Cua Viet River RAD 112 carried out extensive patrol and escort missions. This ATC cruises close to shore to check out suspicious signs of enemy activity. (US Navy)

(Above) The Navy dispatched the three PACVs they had under evaluation in the Mekong Delta to I Corps for evaluation under different conditions. This PACV is coming alongside a dock after a patrol up the Perfume. (US Navy)

(Right) The crews of these PBRs bring down the American flags for the last time prior to turning over their boats to the South Vietnamese. (US Army)

effort to 'pacify' the region and drive out the remnants of the NVA and *VC* forces. However, on the Cua Viet River, the NVA launched a renewed effort to close the waterway to allied traffic. Marines tried to secure the shoreline against these attacks but the elusive guerrillas still managed to continue the attacks. This kept the Dong Ha unit on the defensive, and as NVA efforts increased, more minesweeping vessels had to be assigned to augement the LCM-6s. These new additions included three 57 foot fast MSBs from Minedivision 113 which were much better equipped to handle the mine threat on the Cua Viet than the converted landing craft. With these additional boats, the situation was gradually turned and by mid-1969 attacks along the Cua Viet River had been successfully contained. However, constant patrolling was still continued since the rivers proximaty to the DMZ and Laos gave the communists the opportunity to quickly stage attacks if they felt allied forces were becoming lax.

Minesweepers

Early in the war the *Viet Cong* carried out a number of attacks against both military and commercial vessels using a variety of explosives and mines. A US escort carrier, being used as an aircraft transport, was sunk at the Saigon dock by charges placed on her hull by VC sappers. On the river leading to Saigon a number of cargo ships were damaged by mines detonated from the shore, while on the smaller canals and streams the Vietnamese Navy lost several junks and RAG boats to similar devices. Following the carrier incident, increased harbor surveillance cut down on attacks of this nature but throughout the war enemy swimmers remained a threat, not only to moored ships, but also to shore and river facilities*.

To counter the enemy's mining effort on the main rivers, the US sent four 57 foot wooden hulled minesweepers (MSBs) to Vietnam in early 1966. These boats of Mine Squadron 11 were designated Detachment Alfa and arrived on the Long Tau river in March of 1967. Assigned to Game Warden forces, Detachment Alpha operated under Task Group 116.4 with its headquarters in Saigon. Working alongside of Vietnamese units the American crews swept the Long Tau daily to keep it clear of enemy mines. Normally, the Vietnamese were responsible for the area from Saigon south to Nha Be while the US detachment covered the stretch of the Long Tau from Nha Be to the South China Sea.

Both the Americans and *Viet Cong* realized quite early that these minesweepers were extremely important if the lifeline to Saigon was to be kept open. The US Navy responded by doubling the number of MSBs deployed on the Long Tau within a year of the arrival of Detachment Alfa. For their part the communists increased the frequency of attacks against the lightly armed MSBs. 15 February 1967 was a particularly bad day for the minesweepers. Using mines, rockets, recoilless rifles, and automatic weapons the VC sank one minesweeper (MSB-45), severely damaged another (MSB-49), and hit two others; two sailors were killed and sixteen were wounded, but despite these the unit was sweeping the river the next day. The

During the 1968 Tet offensive, VC sappers, using scuba gear purchased at a local P.X. blew up a major bridge in Hue.

ferocity of these attacks showed just how much the minesweepers were hurting the *VC*'s effort. To counter these attacks, increased PBR and helicopter support was provided while the newly constituted Mobile Riverine Force conducted a series of sweeps along the Long Tau to root out the guerrilla units.

The communists also tried mining the Cua Viet and Perfume rivers in I Corps, and being only a short distance from North Vietnam, it was much easier for the enemy to transport mines to these rivers. Requests from the Marines in late 1967 prompted the Navy to assign five LCM-6s converted to minesweepers for use on the Perfume River in conjunction with a detachment of PBRs. Coverage for the Cua Viet River was provided by a riverine division, minus its ASPBs, whose ATCs had been fitted with minesweeping gear. In mid-1968 these minesweeping ATCs were replaced by five converted LCM-6s which were better equipped for minesweeping duty. Eventually, the Cua Viet force was supplemented by three MSBs from Da Nang harbor, whose main responsibility was to keep the LST turning basin at Cua Viet swept of mines.

While these changes were going on up north, reorganization was taking place in the south. Detachment Alfa was increased in strength and recommissioned as Mine Division 112 during the early spring of 1968. Following this Mine Division 113 was created from various assets in the Rung Sat zone. These two units, operating both MSBs and MSMs, effectively contained the mine threat on the Long Tau River. As a result of this the *Viet Cong* began a more active campaign against moored ships using limpet mines carried by swimmers. A number of moored ships and barges were sunk or damaged by these attacks, but increased vigilance on the part of security forces cut down the success of these attacks.

While the communists occasionally made special efforts on the Long Tau and Cua Viet Rivers, notably at the end of 1968 and into early 1969, constant patrolling by the various minesweeping units near Saigon and in I Corps kept both rivers open to traffic. These forces had to be on constant alert since the enemy was always quick to try some new or unorthodox way to lay mines. To counter these attempts, US sailors replied with their own ingenious solutions in this deadly battle of wits. Despite their best efforts, the NVA and *VC* were unable to stop the flow of men and materials up the rivers, and although the cost was often high, the crews of the minesweepers never failed to keep the waterways open.

HAL-3

While Task Force 116 was formally established in December of 1965, it was some four months before the first PBRs and Swift boats actually began operating along the delta waterways. Their first few engagements taught some hard learned lessons, among which was the need for air support to

To provide bases of operations each of the LSTs assigned to TF 116 was equipped to handle a Detachment of two UH-1 Hueys. This UH-1B gunship takes off from the helicopter deck of Harnett County (LST 821) for a strike against the Viet Cong. These initial Hueys were loaned to the Navy by the 197th AHC until the Navy could procure its own choppers. (US Navy)

counter enemy firepower. While the PBRs and Swift boats carried .50 caliber machine guns, grenade launchers, mortars and other light weapons, they were found to be no match for dug in *Viet Cong* forces with rocket launchers and recoilless rifles. This was brought home during a firefight near Can Tho when PBRs were hit by concealed 57mm recoilless rifles and could not suppress this heavy fire with the weapons on board.

The results of this and other early engagements were reported to naval headquarters in Saigon where the assistant chief-of-staff, Captain John Sheppard saw the reports. After analyzing these reports, he proposed that if the river patrols were to operate effectively they would need air support, specially assigned helicopter gunships. However despite the logic of this and the obvious need of such support, there were problems in organizing such a force. The primary obstacles were the lack of trained Navy aircrews and the lack of helicopters in-country. After discussions with the Army a temporary solution was worked out whereby the 197th Aviation Helicopter Company (197th AHC) provided eight Bell UH-1B gunships to the Navy until they could acquire their own.

Aircrews, however, were harder to come by, but eventually the Navy decided to use personnel from Helicopter Combat Support Squadron One (HC-1) based at Imperial Beach California. This Squadron was essentially a non-combat support unit which had worked mainly in the search and rescue role off of aircraft carriers. Naval authorities felt that these crews could be quickly retrained on the gunships, eliminating the need to wait until new crews could be procured from flight school.

Once this decision was made, volunteers were called for and four detachments of eight pilots and an equal number of aircrewmen were formed. Each detachment was to be equipped with two Army supplied UH-1Bs, which were already in Vietnam. These were the first steps in the process which eventually resulted in the first Navy helicopter attack squadron. By late June of 1966 the lead element, Detachment 29, was ready to ship out. It arrived in Vietnam at the beginning of July under the command of Lieutenant Commander William Rockwell and immediately began training with the 197th AHC. Classes in tactics, maintenance, avionics and airframe characteristics were held daily. Following these classes, familiarization flights and practice missions were flown until the Army instructors were convinced that the Navy personnel were ready. By late summer all four detachments were judged combat ready and on 14 August, the crews moved to the USS Tortuga (LSD 26) for transfer to their assigned bases. A month later, on 19 September, four Navy Detachments (two helicopters each), took over support of TF 116 from Army units.

During their initial deployment the four Detachments were spread out to cover as wide an area as their limited numbers would allow. One two helicopter Detachment, along with the unit's headquarters was located at Vung Tau on the coast, becoming officially known as 'HC-1 Detachment, Vung Tau'. Unofficially the unit was nicknamed 'Rowell's Rats' (exactly how this name came about has yet to be discovered). A second Detachment operated out of Nha Be, a little south of Saigon in the Rung Sat area, a third Detachment was situated toward the center of the Mekong Delta at the river

A Seawolf Huey and the various weapons it carried. Not shown are the .30 and .50 caliber machineguns carried by some ships to counter the VC's increased anti-aircraft defenses which began to be encountered in the mid-1960s. The Seawolf insignia is carried on the nose and NAVY on the Boom. Some helicopters carried the words UNITED STATES NAVY in black on the boom early in the war. (US Navy via Cressman)

town of Vinh Long, and the fourth Detachment was stationed aboard the USS Comstock (LSD-19), which cruised off the coast. These deployment locations were used until the four specially modified LSTs began arriving in early November of 1966. These LSTs were equipped to provide fuel, munitions, and maintenance facilities for the two UH-1Bs and quarters for the eight aircrews of a detachment. Three of the four LSTs were always on line while the fourth was undergoing replenishment or repair. They operated along the Bassac, Co Chien, and Ham Luong rivers and provided a mobile base from which gunship operations could be carried out.

During this early period the four Detachments took part in numerous actions against the elusive guerrilla forces. On 31 October, they teamed up with PBRs against a *VC* sampan fleet of seventy-five junks on the My Tho river. During a three hour running battle over fifty of the junks were sunk and a large number of enemy troops killed. In mid-December another *VC* force was engaged on the My Tho when PBRs ran into heavy fire from fortified positions along the river's edge. Navy gunships were called in to provide support

A detachment of two Hueys operated from this barge at Nha Be. The nearest UH-1 has a .50 caliber machinegun mounted in the starboard door gunner's position. (US Navy)

A UH-1B patrols along a canal in the Mekong Delta in search of the VC. Besides supporting the PBRs HAL-3 also carried out sorties in search of enemy targets of opportunity both during the day and at night. (Bell Helicopter)

and touched off a huge explosion during a firing run. In addition the gunships were also credited with killing fifteen guerrillas and destroying twenty-eight sampans. Such actions became commonplace as Navy crews gained experience and began flying more and more missions in support of the expanding river forces. By early 1967 steps were underway to make the Detachments into a full fledged squadron. This took place on 1 April 1967 when HAL-3 was officially commissioned at its Vung Tau Headquarters. It was the first Navy Squadron ever to be activated in a combat zone.

The upgrading to squadron status brought an influx of men, material, and responsibility. UH-1Bs were received from the 1st Cavalry Division to supplement the original complement of eight Hueys, and additional aircrews and ground support personnel arrived to man them. These increases allowed the squadron to form three more Detachments and expand the area the squadron covered. By the end of 1967 a total of twenty-two gunships were on hand and the various elements were stationed at the following locations:

Detachment	Location
1	Jennings County (LST 846)
2	Nha Be
3	Vinh Long
4	Garrett County (LST 786)
5	Harnett County (LST 821)
6	Dong Tam
7	Binh Thuy

To keep these seven Detachments on line with their fourteen helicopters took a tremendous effort on the part of the ground crews. The remaining eight Hueys of HAL-3 were under constant maintenance in order to keep up the units strength at a full fourteen machines and this was no small accomplishment considering that the majority of the machines already had a great deal of flight time before the army turned them over to the Navy. In addition, since replacements parts had been hard to get at times, many of these UH-1s had received unofficial field modifications by Army personnel to keep them flying. This of course created nightmare maintenance conditions, but despite such obstacles Navy ground crews kept the maximum number of Hueys in the air.

By the end of 1967 things were looking up for HAL-3. With over a year's combat experience under its belt the squadron had become combat seasoned. HAL-3 had learned valuable lessons in that year and proved it could adapt to the constantly changing tactics of the VC and NVA. During this period the squadron officially adopted the name 'Seawolves'. This name had originally been coined by the Army instructors that trained the original four detachments. During early operations the various elements had used 'Seawolves' as its radio call sign and it was only a matter of time until the Hueys of HAL-3 began carrying a large stylized wolf painted on their nose.

Throughout 1967 HAL-3 took part in a great number of varied operations. While their primary job was to support the river forces, Seawolves also provided cover to major land and river operations in the delta region and gave assistance to downed Army helicopters. In addition it carried out medivac operations when the need arose. Squadron personnel experimented with a variety of armament to increase their gunships' efficiency. In the face of growing enemy ground fire, the hand-held M60 machine gun at the door gunner position was replaced with different combinations of .30 and .50 caliber guns to increase the Huey's stand off range. Some gunships flew with a twin .30 caliber mount in place of one of the M-60s while others carried a single .50 caliber machine gun. But while these machine guns provided the necessary range increase, they constantly needed to be reloaded, and many crews disliked them. All three armament combinations were used until the Squadron stood down.

In early 1968, when the *Tet* offensive was launched, the Seawolves helped to hold various delta towns against the surprise attack. Once the communist offensive was blunted the squadron went back to its original mission and helped to retake ground lost during 'Tet'. In late 1968 the Seawolves took part in OPERATION SEALORDS as a blocking force. Some Detachments were shifted closer to Cambodia to help cut the flow of supplies from the 'sanctuaries' there. The Seawolves flew missions in support of ARVN units scattered throughout the delta who quickly came to respect the ability of the Navy gunship crews. HAL-3's response time was outstanding, due in part to the concept of the two-ship element mode of operation. In addition the Seawolves became proficient in flying night missions and often mounted extended night patrols over the rivers and canals in support of PBRs and ARVN forces, or to interdict *VC* water traffic.

The year of 1969 brought about a number of changes in organization, strength, and assignments. A new squadron headquarters and maintenance facility was completed at Binh Thuy early in the year and the squadron's headquarters moved from Vung Tau. Additional UH-1Bs and newer 'C' models became available to the Navy as the Army began taking delivery of

Seawolves also supported Vietnamese Naval forces in the Delta region. This UH-1 covers the advance of two Vietnamese RAG boats moving up a small stream. In such close conditions air support was vital if the boats were not to blunder into an enemy ambush. (US Navy via Cressman)

Hueys were kept on alert in case trouble arose for the river units. The crew of this ship scramble in response to a call for help from two PBRs caught in a VC ambush. The makeshift revetment protected the copter from VC mortar fire. (US Navy)

the new AH-1G Cobra gunship, which resulted in an increase in strength from twenty-two to thirty-three Hueys. HAL-3 also took over the job of a navy utility helicopter detachment known as AIRCOFAT which was based at Saigon. To carry out this additional work HAL-3 received newer UH-1Ls and formed a detachment known as the 'SEALORDS' at Binh Tuy. This small utility detachment carried out liaison duties, mail runs, passenger transportation, supply missions, and SEAL insertions. Later in 1970 additional UH-1Ls were received; eventually all of the Navy UH-1Ls were armed to supplement regular gunships. By the end of 1970 the Navy's helicopter force in the Mekong Delta had reached full strength.

HAL-3 had provided extensive gunship support to the riverines but even with the recent increase in strength the Seawolves were stretched far too thin. A new fixed wing squadron, VAL-4, equipped with OV-10 Broncos was sent to supplement the Seawolves. Early in 1970 HAL-3 Detachments moved closer to the Cambodian border to help cut down on communist infiltration. Unfortunately, when a particular route was closed to the communists they simply switched to another route, lack of numbers prevented HAL-3 from effectively preventing infiltration from Cambodia. In May the Seawolves took part in the invasion of Cambodia. The Naval portion of the Cambodian operation was code named 'TRAN HUNG DAO XI'. HAL-3 encountered little resistance. Detachment 8, aboard the Hunterdon County (LST 838), was responsible for the main support of the Naval forces, while Detachment 9 served as backup and Detachment 5 was held in reserve. As the invasion progressed both the back up and reserve Detachments were called in, as were two additional Detachments, 3 and 4. Elements of the Sealords were also brought in to fly a variety of missions. For political reasons American forces were pulled out of Cambodia at the end of June, with HAL-3 resuming its normal duties in the delta for the remainder of the year with little significant change in operations. A few of the newer C model Hueys were received along with three HH-1K Huey trainers. By year's end the squadron had thirty-seven Hueys on strength, twenty-seven UH-1Bs, two UH-1Cs, four UH-1Ls, and two HH-1Ks. With this additional strength attempts were made to expand operations further into the delta and along the coast, particularly in the Gulf of Thailand.

This expansion of the Seawolves increased the squadron's contact with enemy forces and resulted in high communist losses. Early in 1971, a further responsibility was given to the squadron when Detachment 4 began operating north of Saigon and Detachment 6 carried out flights in support of the Army's 1st and 25th Division's riverine forces near Phu Cuong.

But even as HAL-3s responsibilities were *increased* steps were underway to redeploy the unit. In 1970 ARVN observers had begun flying with the Seawolves acting as interpreters during communication with Vietnamese units. Then, during July of 1971 Vietnamese Air Force (VNAF) personnel began arriving for indoctrination and familiarization training with the unit. Already qualified as helicopter aircrew, the VNAF personnel were now to receive training in riverine tactics. After training, some of these VNAF crews eventually were attached to the Seawolves and flew combat missions with them. Through the remainder of 1971, HAL-3 continued to fly support for the Vietnamese Army, the Vietnamese Navy and for the few US units still operating in the area, mainly SEALs. It also updated its UH-1Cs to M standards with newer, more powerful engines.

As 1972 approached, orders came down for the Seawolves to prepare to stand down. At Binh Thuy on 26 January 1972 HAL-3 officially ceased operations. This marked the end of five long years of hard work throughout the Mekong Delta and adjacent areas. While statistics could be cited to show how effective the Seawolves were against the *VC* and NVA, perhaps the best testimony to HAL-3's outstanding performance can be summed up in the words of a decorated PBR sailor. Of the Seawolves he commented, "They only had one fault — there was never enough of them."

A strike by Seawolves against a large motorized VC launch and some smaller junks. In the first photo (Top Left) a Huey can be seen just off center making a firing run on the target. The last photo (Bottom) shows the Huey circling the target area while the motorized launch burns and begins to sink. Such strikes helped destroy the guerrilla supply network in the delta and made it difficult for the VC to adequately support their forces. (US Navy via Cressman)

VAH-21

During 1967, the Navy realized that an aircraft was needed to interdict the various waterways of the Mekong Delta at night. Since the Air Force had had a great deal of success with their gunship program, the Navy decided to use the same approach. The aircraft chosen for the job was the P-2V Neptune, which was in the process of being phased out of patrol work in favor of the more advanced Lockheed P-3 Orion. In 1967 four SP-2H Neptunes were modified for this role by installing numerous miniguns mounted at various angles and replacing the MAD boom in the tail with a 20mm turret. In addition, the Neptunes also carried a Night Observation Scope, AN/PQ-92 search radar FLIR and LLLTV sensors, Side Looking Airborne Radar, Real Time IR sensors, Moving Target Indicator, Digital Integrated Attack and Navigation Equipment, and a Black Crow truck ignition sensor. Optional weapons loads included mini-gun pods, 500 pound general purpose bombs, and incendiary weapons. Later, a 40mm grenade launcher was also mounted in the bomb bay.

After evaluation during 1967, the four Neptune gunships, under the designation AP-2H, formed VAH-21 at Cam Rahn Bay in 1968. During the fall of 1968 the four gunships flew over 200 night missions against communist road and river traffic in the delta area. With their various radars and sensors, the Neptunes were usually able to hit a truck or small river craft with a high degree of accuracy. The most effective weapon carried by the Neptune gun-

Navy SP.2H Gunships (Neptunes), while few in number, were very effective in the field. Used almost exclusively at night they were painted in three shades of gray. (Sullivan)

ships were the twin 20mm cannons in the tail. Using a special 'sniper' scope the gunner was able to track a target with incendiary rounds, and usually scored a hit. Unfortunately the four aircraft could only do so much. No new aircraft were received, and in the spring of 1969 the unit was decommissioned. The four aircraft were returned to the US where eventually all but one were cut up for scrap. The one is now on display at the Pima County Air Museum.

PACV

One of the most unusual craft employed by the navy in Vietnam was the Patrol Air Cushion Vehicle (PACV), or Hovercraft. Produced by Bell Aerosystems of Buffalo, New York, the PACV was given the official designation SK-5 though this was rarely used. Described as one-third airplane, one-third helicopter, and one-third boat, the Hovercraft zoomed over the water atop a captured bubble of air four feet thick, held inside the Hovercraft's inflated rubber skirts. This air bubble was produced by a seven foot fan mounted under the hull and turned by a General Electric LM-100 gas turbine engine similar to the one powering the UH-1 Huey helicopter. The PACV could skim over the water at speeds of up to 60 knots. In addition it had the capability of clearing five foot waves, four foot solid walls, six foot vegetation, five foot earthmounds and twelve foot ditches. Steering was accomplished by means of a combination rudder and elevator system mounted in the slipstream of the propeller. The PACV was armed with both .50 caliber machine guns and 40mm cannons.

Three of these craft were deployed to Vietnam in May of 1966 with PACV Division 107 for evaluation by both Game Warden (inland waterways) and Market Time (coastal waters). Operating out of Cat Lo with TF 116 the Hovercraft carried out patrols in the Rung Sat working with PBRs. Following this, the PACVs were attached to the USS Tortuga (LSD-26) to work with TF 115 along the coast of Vietnam, sharing the Tortuga's facilities with PBRs of River Patrol Squadron 512 and Army Hueys of the 145th Aviation Detachment (later replaced by the helicopters of the Seawolves). While some mechanical problems arose during these early trials, the hovercraft performed well in both the river patrol and coastal patrol roles, though they did not experience any significant contact with the enemy.

In November the chance came to give the PACVs an opportunity to par-

PACVs were deployed to Vietnam during the spring of 1966 for evaluation by both Game Warden and Market Time forces. The first operations were with TF 116 out of Cat Lo alongside of PBRs in the Rung Sat. This PACV moves over a reed covered swamp in search of the elusive guerrillas. (US Navy)

ticipate in a combat situation. North of the Mekong Delta near the Cambodian border was a thirty by seventy mile stretch of marsh known as the 'Plain of Reeds', which was used by the VC as a rest and training area. Naval authorities decided that this would be an ideal place to test the hovercraft's combat capability. Working out of the ARVN air boat base at Moc Hoa with Green Berets, the hovercraft took part in OPERATION QUAI VAT. Quai Vat in Vietnamese means 'monster' and this nickname was given to the PACVs due to their massive shape, noise, and the dust or mist they kicked up while moving. PACV crews soon began using 'monster' as their call sign. To further exploit the psychological effect that the hovercraft had on Vietnamese peasants, the sailors painted huge shark mouths and slanted eyes on the front skirts of the hovercraft. QUAI VAT which ended in December, was moderately successful. Twenty-three guerrillas were killed and eleven prisoners were taken, and seventy sampans and seventy-one structures of various sizes were destroyed. While not extraordinary, these results did demonstrate that the PACV could operate under combat conditions.

After the initial trials, the PACVs were cleared for combat with Game Warden forces. They operated throughout 1967 and into 1968 in concert with PBRs and Seawolf UH-1Bs. In early 1968, I Corps requested naval assets for use on the Perfume and Cua Viet rivers. Naval headquarters at Saigon decided to assign the hovercraft to this area to test them in a different environment. Arriving in June, the division was assigned to the Hue River Security Group of Task force Clearwater. Working with elements of the 101st Air-

(Above) Following trials with Game Warden forces the PACVs moved to the USS Tortuga (LSD 26) for trials with Market Time forces along the coast. The crew of this PACV check a small junk for arms or supplies which might be destined for the Viet Cong. (US Navy)

(Below) After their combat test during OPERATION QUAI VAT the PACVs took the call sign 'Monster' and their crews painted sharkmouths on the crafts' bow. The sight of this machine with the gaping mouth frightened more than a few Vietnamese peasants into cooperating with the Navy crews. (US Navy)

borne (Airmobile) Division, they were used to track down guerrillas who had evaded the paratroopers by taking to small sampans in the marshy areas around Hue. When the VC tried to escape by going ashore, the hovercraft surprised the guerrillas by coming ashore after them. The PAVCs performed well in the I Corps area but by the middle of 1969 the three craft were beginning to show the wear and tear of almost three years of continuous use. The Navy decided to retire them, and during the summer of 1969 the PACVs were pulled out of service, being replaced by Army Air Cushion Vehicles (ACVs).

Throughout their deployment the PACVs had done a creditable job but exhibited characteristics which mitigated against their being used in large numbers. They could not maneuver as well as the PBRs, nor were they as quiet. On the plus side, however, they were much faster and could go over obstacles which would stop PBRs. The main factor which hurt the PACVs was their price. Each one cost nearly a million dollars compared to ninety thousand for a new PBR. As such the hovercraft were completely uneconomical when compared with the smaller patrol boat, and even with their unique characteristics, they were not considered to be a superior craft to the PBRs.

VAL-4

The helicopters of HAL-3 were doing an exceptional job in supporting ground and river units in the delta, but lacked sufficient numbers to adequately cover the region. Even after the Army increased the number of Hueys for use by the Navy from twenty-two to thirty-three in April of 1969, it still was not enough. Another problem was the increasing ability of the VC to hit the Huey with ground fire. To counter this problem the Army had begun replacing their Huey gunships with the new AH-1 Cobra gunship, a heavily

A PACV with a ferocious grin. The craft carried a variety of machine guns and grenade launchers and could skim over the water at speeds approaching 70 Knots. (US Navy)

armed and armored gunship specifically designed for the ground support role, but since they were in short supply the Navy was unable to procure any of them.

To solve these problems the Navy decided to deploy the North American OV-10 Bronco in lieu of obtaining additional Hueys from the Army. The OV-10 had originated as a joint Air Force, Marine, and Navy project to design a lightly armed reconnaissance aircraft specifically tailored for use in the counterinsurgency warfare role. The Marines had been the first to employ the Bronco in Vietnam, and the Air Force quickly followed. Within a short time the OV-10 Bronco had acquired an outstanding reputation for its combat prowess. Those qualities that impressed the Navy most were the Bronco's ordnance carrying capacity, ruggedness, short field performance, speed, and range. The Bronco ideally suited Navy support needs in the Mekong Delta.

In order to get the Bronco into service as quickly as possible the Navy 'borrowed' eighteen aircraft from the Marines to equip both a training unit and an operational squadron. VS-41, based at NAS North Island received four OV-10s to begin training. In January of 1969, VAL-4 was commissioned to take the Bronco into combat. Because this was such a unique squadron for the Navy, emphasis was placed on the training syllabus. Running fifteen weeks, the training course emphasized gunnery, ordnance delivery, forward air control procedures, reconnaissance, close coordination with riverine forces, and lastly the crews received sessions in jungle survival in case they were forced down. In March of 1969 VAL-4 deployed, in two eight plane sections, to the airfields at Vung Tau and Binh Thuy.

Upon their arrival, VAL-4 crews immediately began flying support missions for the PBRs along the waterways of the Mekong Delta. Within a short time, the unit suffered its first casualty when a Bronco, piloted by Lieutenant Peter Russell, was hit by ground fire while on patrol. Lt Russell, who had downed a MiG-17 in November of 1966 while flying an A-1 Skyraider, was killed but his backseater was able to bring the aircraft home. The death of this outstanding young officer had a sobering affect on squadron personnel, and they set out with a grim determination to do the job they had been trained to do.

While VAL-4 was primarily responsible for supporting brown water forces in the Mekong Delta, it soon acquired extra duties. These additional assignments included combat air patrols and general reconnaissance in search of targets of opportunity. VAL-4 quickly adopted the nickname and tactical call sign 'Black Ponies', based upon the OV-10's name of Bronco. Within a short time, the Black Ponies established an outstanding reputation for themselves. During their first year of operations they flew over 7500 sorties in all kinds of weather and around the clock. Taking full advantage of the Bronco's load carrying ability, the Ponies struck hard at communist positions throughout the Mekong Delta. Though not able to maneuver as well as the Huey, after locating a target the Bronco made up for it by carrying a far heavier and more varied ordnance load over a much greater range. In particular its ability to carry a variety of rockets and bombs allowed Black Pony crews to more effectively engage enemy targets. In addition these fixed wing

A Black Pony OV-10 Bronco takes off from Vung Tau on a search and destroy mission over the Mekong Delta. The Bronco was well liked by Navy crews for its ruggedness and handling qualities. In addition the plane could carry a wide variety of weapons which gave it great flexibility during ground support missions. (US Navy)

aircraft proved very easy to maintain in the field with VAL-4 achieving a high degree of serviceability.

Throughout its deployment to Vietnam the Black Ponies functioned almost exclusively in the ground attack role. They constantly patrolled over the Mekong Delta and the waterways which crisscrossed it. Enemy troop concentrations, supply dumps, fortified positions, and river craft were hit with a high degree of accuracy. The Broncos proved especially effective in supporting the riverine forces when they ran into an ambush along the rivers or canals. Their speed and rugged construction countered the ever increasing enemy ground fire which was proving extremely hazardous to the Hueys.

The majority of these patrols were flown in a two plane formation. Each eight plane detachment maintained a twenty-four hour, seven day a week scramble alert crew of four pilots and two OV-10s. These alert crews were on call in case allied units needed immediate air support, or if an enemy target was spotted. In addition, single ship reconnaissance flights were flown daily over the Rung Sat Special Zone in search of enemy staging areas. Normally, a Marine air observer was carried in the rear seat as a spotter. When a target was detected the Pony called for assistance and carried out its own attack until reinforcements appeared.

VAL-4 played a particularly important role during the Cambodian invasion. On 6 May 1970 the unit flew support for river forces moving up the Kham Spean River as part of the drive into the Parrot's Beak, a longtime *VC* stronghold west of Saigon. On 8 May, a flotilla of American and Vietnamese riverine craft pushed up the Mekong River in an attempt to open the river to Phnom Pehn, the capitol of Cambodia. The main target of this thrust was the town of Neak Long which had been captured by the *VC* early in May. Neak Long was the site of the ferry over the Mekong River for Route 1, a major overland route to the Cambodian capital. US forces turned back at the twenty-one mile limit set by President Nixon but Vietnamese Naval units pushed on and eventually linked up with an ARVN ground column. During this thrust into Cambodia the Broncos flew continuously in support of the riverine units. At times heavy enemy fire from shore slowed down the forces moving up the rivers but the OV-10s were quick to attack at the first sign of resistance and the advance continued without serious hindrance. The enemy, realizing that they could do little to hold Neak Long, quickly abandoned it, and the town fell to the South Vietnamese on 10 May.

OV-10s of VAL-4 sit in revetments at Vung Tau. The squadron was formed to help supplement the brown water navy's air effort in the Delta. Since the Bronco had been specially designed for counterinsurgency warfare it was an ideal choice. (Wiggs)

Following the Cambodian invasion, US river assets were cut drastically in the Mekong Delta. By September of 1970 there were few river craft manned by wholly American crews. As a result VAL-4 became an airborne quick reaction force. Two plane formations began carrying out patrols over assigned areas, with different aircraft covering an area from dusk to dawn. Most of the missions flown were in support of Vietnamese units and by the end of American involvement in the war over ninety per cent of the Black Pony missions were devoted to this type of patrol.

At the beginning of 1971 VAL-4 started flying support missions for a series of TRAN HUNG DAO OPERATIONS which involved what was left of US Naval forces in country and Vietnamese riverine units. These missions lasted into the early summer of the 1971, but were discontinued when the remaining American operational river craft were turned over to the Vietnamese. When these missions were terminated the Ponies began flying random patrols over the delta as a quick airborne reactionary force for any unit which needed air support on a moments notice. However, this new procedure did not fully utilize the assets of VAL-4 and consequently several other missions were assigned to the squadron. These included cover missions for ARVN supply convoys, visual airborne reconnaissance surveillance (VARS), and navel gunfire spotting.

The cover missions were flown primarily for Vietnamese river craft on supply runs to army positions in the Mekong Delta, particularly in the Bing Thuy-Can Tho area. Prior to this overhead cover, the convoys had often come under attack from small guerrilla bands, but once overhead cover was instituted these attacks fell off dramatically. In the VARS role, OV-10s were used to patrol along the coast to check for infiltration and monitor the performance of Game Warden units. From their beginnings, in September of 1971, to the final sortie in April of 1972, 225 VARS missions were flown. During these flights, an observer from Task Force 115 replaced the VAL-4 rear seater, and gathered the needed information for his command. In a similar vein the naval gunfire assignment entailed flying a marine observer along the coast who spotted targets for ships and coordinated their fire with ground units. Normally, a single plane flew these missions, of which one or two were scheduled per day.

Throughout the remainder of 1971, the Black Ponies flew numerous sorties throughout the delta region in support of Vietnamese Army and Naval units. The squadron proved particularly valuable as a quick reaction force when support was needed for an embattled outpost or a pinned down infantry unit. Numerous times VAL-4 was able to break up enemy attacks and save a beleaguered post or prevent a trapped infantry unit from being overrun. By the end of 1971 over 7,000 sorties had been flown against enemy targets. During these missions, over 2400 NVA and *VC* troops were credited to the squadron while only one aircraft was lost. However, it had been decided by higher authorities to redeploy the unit stateside for deactivation as part of the American withdrawal program. In early 1972 squadron personnel began to rotate back to the US, but VAL-4 continued to fly missions. In the first three months of 1972 it flew over 2000 sorties, but on 31 March, the Black Ponies flew their last combat mission when a strike was flown against *VC* positions near the 21st ARVN Division. On 1 April 1972 the squadron officially stood down at Binh Tuy, the last Navy squadron in-country to do so. Three days later the crews flew their OV-10s to Cubi Point in the Phillippines, where, on 10 April 1972, VAL-4 was officially deactiviated, ending the history of one of the most unique US Navy squadrons to serve in the Vietnam war.

Ordnance was mixed to get optimum results during a sortie. In addition to the sponson machine guns, this OV-10 carries a mini gun pod, two sets of 5 inch Zuni rockets, and a 2.75 inch launcher. The use of the Black Pony insignia originated when the squadron first deployed to Vietnam. Later the insignia was moved to the tail and then was reapplied to the forward fuselage while often being retained on the tail. (Wiggs)

The OV-10 Bronco proved easy to maintain and VAL-4 was able to achieve a high sortie rate. The squadron left Vietnam in early 1972 after almost three years of flying support for US and Vietnamese brown water units. (Wiggs)

A two-ship element of VAL-4 flies low over the delta in search of targets of opportunity. The outer wing stations are fitted with two shot Zuni rocket racks. This weapon was used frequently because of its range and high explosive charge. (US Navy)

SEALS

One of the least known Navy activities in Vietnam were operations by SEAL teams. These Navy commandos took their name from the elements in which they were trained to fight — Sea, Air, and Land, hence the name SEAL. Highly skilled in underwater demolition, scuba diving, parachuting, hand-to-hand combat, and proficient with a variety of weapons, the SEALs usually worked under the direction of TF 116 throughout most of the war. The SEALs carried out a number of clandestine missions inside North Vietnam, including reconnaissance missions into Haiphong Harbor itself.

The first detachments, from SEAL Team 1, deployed to Vietnam in February of 1966, beginning operations in the Rung Sat Special Zone. Their primary mission in the Rung Sat was to infiltrate enemy territory and carry out hit and run raids against the *VC*. Operating in three man elements, the SEALS were usually inserted under cover of darkness to carry out their assignment, after which they proceeded to a rendezvous point for pickup. Normally, a 'Mike' boat, a heavily armored riverine craft, or PBR was used for the insertion and pickup, but later in the war Boston Whalers, STAB (Seal Team Assault Boat) craft, and LSSCs (Light Seal Support Craft) were used for these duties. Helicopters were also employed on certain occasions, and were often used to carry small sampans which the SEALS used to infiltrate closely guarded enemy areas disguised as local inhabitants.

During their first year in Vietnam, the SEALS performed extraordinarily well, killing hundreds of *Viet Cong*, while suffering minimal casualties themselves. As a result of their performance, the number of SEAL personnel in 1967 was greatly increased and they were given additional assignments. While their main function continued to be small unit raids, the SEALs were also used to spearhead river operations in the Mekong Delta and carry out special reconnaissance patrols for larger units. During some of these operations the SEALs were teamed with their Army counterparts, the Green Berets, with whom there existed a good natured rivalry. As part of these reconnaissance missions, the SEALs sometimes set up surveillance posts along the various waterways to determine which were being used by the guerrillas. This data allowed US and Vietnamese officials to get a picture of how widespread enemy infiltration was in the region.

In 1968, a number of new assignments were given to the expanded SEAL force. In addition to their normal duties, the SEALs began working as advisors with both US and Vietnamese units, schooling them in the use of SEAL tactics to help them counter the elusive guerrillas. They also carried out operations with the MACV Special Operations Group (MACV/SOG) which led to secret missions inside North Vietnam and Cambodia. The SEALs also worked with Provincial Reconnaissance Units (PRUs) whose job it was to kill or capture *VC* leaders and political officers inside Vietnam. Code named the 'Phoenix' Program, this type of operation generated intense opposition from the US news media and anti-war movement which viewed it as a 'murder for hire' program. This criticism had to be taken with a grain (or full bag) of salt since these same groups seemed to see nothing wrong with the communists carrying out political assassinations or using supposed 'neutral' Cambodia and Laos as staging areas for their raids into South Vietnam. The 'Phoenix' Program proved particularly successful in the delta area, and resulted in severe losses to the *Viet Cong*. A large part of the credit for its success (which they of course could not receive) was due to the work that individual SEALs performed while assigned to the program.

In 1969, while other Naval forces were preparing for withdrawal from Vietnam, SEAL strength was increasing. SEAL Team Two, with three detachments (Golf, Bravo, and Echo) received two additional platoons in late 1969, to cover the additional duties assigned to them. Though many of their duties revolved around the PRU program and the training of the South Vietnamese, elements were assigned to work with TF 115 for coastal surveillance work. Many teams integrated Vietnamese personnel within their structure to provide them with experience in SEAL operations. These Vietnamese members often brought with them a knowledge of the area that the team worked in and provided valuable information during combat missions.

The crew of this STAB makes a high speed run during a sweep near the Cambodian border. The boat is armed with M-60 machineguns and a 40mm automatic grenade launcher. (US Navy)

Without a doubt one of the finest groups of fighting men in Vietnam, the SEALS compiled a fantastic record during the six years they were deployed in Southeast Asia. This group of SEALs board a Strike Assault Boat (STAB) for transportation to an ambush site. Note the variety of weapons and uniforms which the men wear. Normally the choice of weapons was left up to the individual SEAL unless mission requirements dictated otherwise. (US Navy)

The crews of these STABs ready their boats for a mission after dark. Boat Support Unit One provided the most common means of transportation for the Seal Teams though on occasion PBRs and UH-1s were also used. Note the different types of armament the various boats carry and the amount of extra gear the crews have scattered about. (US Navy)

In 1970, however, the withdrawal caught up with the SEALs. Slowly, they began to turn over more and more of their duties to the Vietnamese. Despite this, operations were still carried out. In late 1970, SEAL personnel teamed up with Vietnamese militiamen to raid a *VC* prison compound, rescued nineteen Vietnamese, and captured two of the *VC* guards along with weapons, supplies, and documents. Operations of this type decreased in 1971, but some clandestine missions into Cambodia took place during the closing stages of the war to monitor the communist build up in the border sanctuaries.

As the US pullout accelerated in 1972, SEAL strength was cut drastically. The few remaining SEAL personnel in Vietnam worked mainly in the advisory role until the end of the war. The final tally for the six years of operations came to over 600 *VC* confirmed dead along with an additional 300 almost certainly killed. In addition the number of captured guerrillas and detained suspects numbered well over 1000. Yet, these figures were achieved by a force that never numbered over 200 men and suffered less than a dozen casualties over their six year deployment. Unfortunately, due to the nature of their work most of the records of SEAL operations are still classified which makes it difficult to give an accurate account of their work. A member of the Australian Special Air Service (SAS), one of the elite military units in the world, had this to say about the SEALs he worked with in Vietnam. "They were the best, bar none".

MOBILE RIVERINE FORCE (TF-117)

By 1966 US troops had been committed in large numbers to three of the four corps areas of Vietnam. Only in IV Corps, the Mekong Delta region, were there no large numbers of American troops. This was due to three major factors. First, though the delta was a major population and food center, the military situation was not as critical as in the other corps areas. Second, due to the density of the population, there was no available tracts of land where a large military installation could be constructed without dislocating large numbers of people. And finally, the numerous rivers, streams and canals which dissected the delta severely restricted ground movement; US planners were reluctant to commit US troops to such an environment until they found a way to overcome the mobility problem.

However, in 1966, there was a strong desire on the part of the US Army to insert troops in the Mekong Delta to counter growing communist strength. In March of 1966 a joint planning committee of Army and Navy personnel drew up tentative plans for the establishment of a Mekong Delta Mobile Afloat Force (MDMAF). This proposal was further detailed during the summer, and by September plans had reached the implementation stage. On 1 September, the first administrative unit of the new organization was commissioned at the Navy Amphibious Base in Coronado, California. Shortly after this, the unit received the designation Task Force 117 (TF-117), and was code named the Mobile Riverine Force. (MRF).

As originally envisioned the MRF would support an infantry brigade and an artillery battalion using a variety of modified landing craft, support ships, and specially designed assault boats. In essence this strike unit would be, a self contained amphibious assault force, complete with all support elements except aircraft. The ideal choice for the ground component would have been the Marines who were specialists in amphibious warfare, but unfortunately the Leathernecks were already heavily committed in I Corps. Instead, a brigade from the 9th Infantry Division was chosen as the infantry component of the Mobile Riverine Force.

The Naval component of TF 117 was made up of a wide variety of ships and boats. The first unit, River Assault Squadron 9 (RAS 9), consisted of four APBs, two LSTs, twenty-six ATCs five Monitors, two CCBs, one Refueler, and sixteen ASPBs.

River Assault Flotilla One

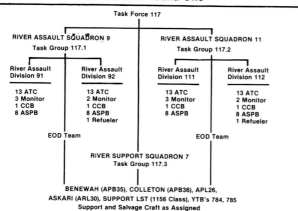

The small craft were equally divided between River Assault Divisions 91 and 92 (RAD 91 and RAD 92) while the support ships formed River Support Squadron 7 (RSS 7). Eventually another six divisions would be added to TF 117. Except for the ASPB which was newly designed, all these craft were basically standard navy vessels modified for use with the MRF.

The first operations by Task Force 117 were undertaken in co-operation with Vietnamese Riverine units. These US troops return to base onboard a Vietnamese Monitor after a two day operation. The turret mounts a 40mm cannon while on the bridge there are a number of machine gun mounts. (US Navy)

The first elements of the Mobile River Force reached Vietnam on 7 January 1967 when the USS Whitfield County (LST 1169) docked at Vung Tau. Training began immediately with the 2nd Brigade of the 9th Infantry Division, This unit, in preparation for assignment to the Mobile Riverine Force, had gotten rid of their tanks, trucks, APCs and jeeps since there would obviously be little need for them in the Mekong Delta. In addition, some of their heavier artillery was also left behind since most of the necessary fire support would be supplied by the assault boats. Unfortunately, because the initial number of barracks ships could only handle two of the brigade's three infantry battalions and artillery batteries, the remaining units had to operate out of the newly constructed shore facility at Dong Tam until the rest of TF 117's ships were available.

The major problem initially faced by the MRF was the lack of having their own vessels to train on. For the first few months TF 117 used borrowed Vietnamese Navy landing craft and control boats until its own boats began arriving. During this time, the Viet Cong carried out a number of attacks against ships on the Long Tau river. On 15 February 1967 the VC sank one US minesweeper and damaged three others. As a result of these attacks, plans were made to carry out regular search and destroy missions in the Rung Sat zone which bordered the Long Tau, even though the Mobile Riverine Force lacked their own boats. Working with Vietnamese units operations were carried out through March which resulted in a substantial drop in attacks by the communist guerrillas. However despite these efforts the Rung Sat continued to be used by the VC and throughout the war allied forces had to periodically sweep the area to deny the enemy free access to it.

Gradually the MRF built up its strength. However, the number of boats

In contrast with Vietnamese Monitors this American Monitor has a number of significant differences. Although it also carries a 40mm cannon mounted in the turret there is a combination mortar/machine gun mount in the space behind the turret along with a single 20mm and two .50 caliber machine gun turrets atop the superstructure. This particular Monitor is from RAS 91. Note the tubular stretcher attached to the aft side of the superstructure for casualty evacuation. (US Navy)

51

The Command Control Boat (CCB) is similar to the Monitor but carries additional communications gear in lieu of the combination mortar/machine gun mount. This particular CCB is inspecting the two junks in the foreground for possible enemy troops who might try to slip out of the landing area. Once troops were ashore the Riverine craft were responsible for sealing off all water routes to block enemy escape attempts. (US Navy)

needed to fill out the Force's prescribed strength took time to produce and deploy to Vietnam. It was not until 1968 that the full complement of 180 river assault craft was reached, but fortunately, by the summer of 1967 there were enough boats on hand to carry out sustained search and destroy missions. These boats were rather unique vessels, and with one exception, were modified landing craft (LCM-6s).

The main craft of the River Assault Squadron were armored troop carriers (ATCs) which were capable of carrying a full infantry platoon. Armed with a 20mm cannon, two .50 caliber machine guns, and two Mark 18 grenade launchers, plus various hand held weapons, the ATCs not only landed troops, but also resupplied them and provided close-in fire support during operations. Since they were expected to get within close range of enemy forces these boats were well protected with both conventional and 'stand-off' armor. This 'stand off' or bar armor was a series of metal rods a foot or so out from the ATCs hull and upper works and was designed to detonate RPG or recoilless rifle rounds before they hit the structural armor plate. 'Stand-off armor' proved to be very effective against both hand held and crew served weapons used by the *VC*, and significantly reduced casualties and damage when an ATC was hit by enemy fire.

Some armored troop carriers were modified with a helicopter flight deck mounted over the troop wells. This was done initially to provide a platform for helicopters to land on for delivery of supplies and transfer of personnel. Almost immediately, however, the helicopters were pressed into service for casualty evacuation since they were often the only place for a helicopter to land during operations in the Delta. From this conversion came another; some of the armored troop carriers with helicopter pads, designated ATC(H)s, were fitted as battalion aid stations and carried a doctor and either Army or Navy corpsmen. During operations one ATC(H) also carried refrigerated whole blood and there was always a fully equipped operating table ready to perform emergency surgery.

Each river squadron also had an ATC fitted out as a refueler. These carried bladders of *mogas* or *avgas* under the flight deck to refuel the squadron's

Armored Troop Carriers (ATCs) carried the infantry element of the MRF into combat. Unlike a Monitor the ATC retained the ramp in the bow to allow troops to disembark. The overhead awnings atop the troop compartment provided protection from the sun and rain while troops were in transit. (US Navy)

boats, assault craft, and sometimes even helicopters. These refuelers proved indispensable during prolonged operations and pumped huge quantities of fuel to keep the riverine forces on station.

The main fire support vessel of the MRF was the Monitor. They were somewhat similar to the ATC from the stern forward to the troop deck, however, here all similarity ended. In a small open pit forward of the superstructure, an 81mm mortar, similar to those aboard the Swift boats and Coast Guard cutters, was mounted. Forward of this a spoon shaped bow replaced the flat unloading ramp of the ATC. On this new bow was mounted a 40mm cannon (with a co-axial .50 caliber machine gun) enclosed in a turret. The 40mm was the main gun of the riverine forces and it provided a high volume of fire during landing operations. In addition, at least two Mark 18 grenade launchers were carried, along with the individual weapons of the crewmen. Heavily armored, the Monitors often closed to within a few feet of the shore to provide fire support for the troops on shore.

Two Monitors in each squadron were also fitted out as Command Control Boats (CCBs). The only major difference between a regular Monitor and a CCB Monitor was the removal of the mortar in the pit aft of the 40mm turret. In its place a command and control console was fitted which served as the command post for the battalion and task group commanders during an operation. Otherwise the CCB Monitor was identical to a regular monitor and carried out much the same function.

The only boat specially constructed for use by the riverine forces was the Assault Support Patrol Boat (ASPB). In addition to providing fire support the ASPB was also designed to serve as a minesweeper and was fitted with a mine countermeasure chain drag. Lighter and faster than the Monitor, the ASPB was not as heavily armed or armored. It carried a single 20mm cannon and twin .50 caliber machine guns in two turrets, one in the bow, and one atop the superstructure. An 81mm mortar was mounted in the stern and two or more Mark 18 grenade launchers were also carried. The ASPB had a unique exhaust system which emptied out underwater making it the quietest of the riverine boats. Combined, these features allowed the ASPB to be used in a wide variety of roles. Aside from leading the river flotillas it was also employed for ambushes, patrols, special operations, reconnaissance, and escort missions. Later in the war, single or twin .50 caliber machine guns were added to the stern while the forward gun turret had rocket launchers mounted on their sides. Linked to the machine guns the rocket launchers could be trained by elevating or depressing the machine guns and traversing the turret.

Besides these fighting boats, the Mobile Riverine Force had a number of support boats. Two self-propelled barracks ships (APBs), were modified for use in Vietnam. Each was fitted with a flight deck and equipped with air conditioning. Each could accommodate approximately eight hundred troops and provide some support for the river boats. In addition each APB was outfitted with an extensive communications system. The Benewah (APB-35) was equipped to serve as the brigade and flotilla flagship while the Colleton (APB-36) had similar arrangements for battalion and squadron commanders. In late 1967 the Colleton also received hospital facilities for the care of lightly wounded men.

However, since these two barracks ships could not handle all the men of the two infantry battalions, and artillery batteries, another barracks ship, non-propelled, supplemented the Benewah and Colleton*. It could house another 625 men, but being unpowered, it had to be towed from place to

*Five APBs had originally been requested but three were cut from the force by Secretary of Defense McNamara. Fortunately the Navy was able to provide a non-propelled replacement.

place. This hampered the MRF since its movement was relatively slow and created tactical problems for the Riverine forces. Eventually two additional Self-Propelled Barracks Ships, the Mercer (APB-39), and Nieces (APB-40) were added to the Mobile Riverine Force to cut down on this problem.

To service and repair the various riverine boats and landing craft a repair ship was assigned to the support section of the task force. The USS Askari (ARL-30), a converted LST, provided a complete repair facility for the river craft. Cranes onboard could lift boats out of the water and deposit them on Ammi pontoons moored alongside for drydock work. In addition, the Askari also housed Army personnel who worked on weapons, radios, and engines. This ship provided indispensable service and without it the MRF would have been unable to keep its boats in service and carry out operations.

The last major support vessels of Task Force 117 were 1156-class LSTs assigned to the flotilla from the 7th Fleet. These provided additional storage space which was unavailable on the APBs. In this space the LSTs housed supplemental supplies of ammunition, weapons, spare parts, and rations for reprovisioning the riverine forces during prolonged operations. These LSTs were equipped with a flight deck and carried the brigade's helicopter detachment of four H-23s, along with one infantry company. They also supported a River Assault Division.

The final component of the riverine forces were the artillery and helicopter barges developed by the Army. Initially, it was envisioned that artillery would be put ashore to provide the necessary fire support. Very quickly it was discovered that there were few tracts of solid land in the Mekong Delta which could support artillery. To alleviate this problem an Army office had a barge fabricated from sections of pontoons which enabled two 105mm howitzers to fire while anchored next to the shoreline. These barges could also be beached if the tide went out and the artillery could be resighted, allowing the gun crews to keep firing their howitzers after only a slight delay. Helicopters also faced the same problems since there were few areas for them to set down. The ATC(H) provided only a partial solution, and the problem persisted. Similar to the artillery barges, a helicopter barge was developed using sections of pontoons. Each of these helicopter barges could accommodate three Hueys and were equipped with a refueling system which carried 1,500 gallons of JP-4 aviation fuel. Since neither of these barges were self-propelled LCM-8s were used to move them for resupply of fuel and ammunition. These barges provided a quick and inexpensive solution to the problems faced by both artillery batteries and helicopter crews. As a result the MRF did not lack for artillery or helicopter support.

Riverine Operations

RIVER RAIDER I, the search and destroy mission carried out in the Rung Sat during February and March of 1967, was the first joint operation by Army and Navy forces. The Vietnamese Navy had provided some of the craft for use in the campaign since the full American contingent of vessels had not yet arrived. Throughout the spring of 1967 the Mobile Riverine Force gradually built up its strength, and carried out small local operations. During April and May the Kemper County (LST-854), the Benewah (APB-35), and the Colleton (APB-36) arrived in-country and began supporting the riverine craft. In mid-May TF 117 joined with TF 116 (Game Warden) forces to carry out the largest riverine operation by US forces to date in the Rung Sat. This operation also marked the first time that both Task Forces worked together in support of one another.

Shortly after this joint operation was concluded, OPERATION HOPTAC

ATC(H)s were modified with the addition of a small flight deck to allow helicopters to land. Some of these were used as hospital boats and had full operating facilities fitted in the deck well. (US Navy)

XVIII was carried out in the area between the Rach Ba Bau and Rach Tra Tan rivers in IV Corps. Even larger than the Rung Sat operation, it resulted in the first heavy contact with the *Viet Cong*. After landing the infantry, the ATCs, supported by Monitors, blocked off the enemy's line of retreat, and despite fierce fighting the *VC* were unable to escape the net thrown around them. Pressed from all sides they broke and ran, losing over 100 men. Casualties among the infantry and sailors were light and damage to the various river craft was minor. The boats had proven they could stand up to rocket and recoilless rifle fire, even at extremely close range, and their ability to block the *VC*'s escape had been the decisive factor in sealing the fate of the guerrilla force. Without them, the guerrillas would have been able to slip away to fight again.

Shortly after this operation was completed on 2 June, the MRF received a directive from MACV in Saigon, assigned the code name CORONADO to future riverine operations*. Two days later CORONADO I began in Dinh Tuong and Kien Hoa provinces to secure the Cho Gao canal. During the move up river to insert an infantry platoon ATC-112-3, acting as a minesweeper, had a mine detonate under its stern and had to be towed back to the new Army base at Dong Tam. This was the first successful mining of a MRF ship and highlighted the need for a specialized minesweeper. Unfortunately, while most of the remaining modified landing craft arrived during June, the ASPBs were not among them. The lack of these specially designed boats had some effects on operations but other craft were assigned the minesweeping duty until the ASPBs finally reached TF-117. Although without the ASPBs the Mobile Riverine Force was not up to authorized strength, the arrival of the last of the modified LCMs allowed the Navy to return borrowed riverine craft to the Vietnamese Navy without jeopardizing the force's ability to carry out its mission.

Throughout the summer and fall of 1967 the riverine force was constantly on the move. In late June Coronado OPERATION CONCORDIA trapped a *VC* unit of some 400 men near Ap Bac. Together with ARVN units the soldiers and sailors of the MRF killed over 250 of the enemy while losing 46 men. Again the riverine craft helped cut the enemy's line of retreat, and while heavy fire was taken, there were only fifteen sailors wounded during the bat-

*Coronado California, was the site of the Naval Amphibious Base at which most sailors received special training prior to shipping out to Vietnam

This particular landing craft has been converted to a 'rocket boat'. In the deck well are a number of five inch rocket launchers which are used to provide support fire in a general area. Note the additional armor on the stern and gun mounts. (US Navy)

As the war progressed additional field modifications were made to the standard riverine boats to improve their effectiveness and protection. This particular Monitor has had the forward 40mm turret replaced with two flame throwers. Nicknamed 'ZIPPOs', these craft were used to burn away the dense jungle foliage which often grew down to the water's edge. (US Navy)

tle. CONCORDIA II followed at the beginning of July and lasted until 24 July. During this campaign PBRs of TF 116 (Game Warden) assisted the MRF in blocking operations but their limited armor protection hindered their use in the close confines of the small canals where their primary protection, speed, could not be used effectively. At this time the MRF began operating H-23 and UH-1 helicopters off the ATC(H)s which increased the flexibility of the force's reconnaissance and medivac ability. The first of the converted helicopter barges arrived on 22 July and was pressed into service immediately to supplement the ATC(H)s.

From August through October TF 117 carried out a series of operations against the VC in the Rung Sat Special Zone to keep the main shipping channel open. These included CORONADO III (5-17 August), CORONADO VI (11-18 October), and CORONADO VIII (27-29 October). None of these resulted in significant contact with large VC units. Only scattered resistance was encountered but these operations prevented the VC from carrying out attacks on the shipping channel due to this constant probing by the riverine force.

In conjunction with these forays into the Rung Sat the MRF also carried out a number of other operations in the surrounding areas. CORONADO IV (19 August to 9 September) took place south and southwest of Saigon in Long An, Co Cong, and Kien Hoa provinces. Elements of the 506th VC Battalion were encountered and thirty-four of the guerrillas were killed.

The only vessel specifically designed for use by riverine forces was the Assault Support Patrol Boat (ASPB). The turrets housed either a single 20mm cannon or twin .50 caliber machine guns. An 81mm mortar was carried in the stern and grenade launchers were mounted as needed. These craft were also fitted for minesweeping and normally led an assault formation down the river. (US Navy)

Numerous supply and arms caches were also discovered but contact was light. Close on the heels of this came CORONADO V (September 12th to October 8th) in Dinh Tuong and Kien Hoa provinces, southwest of the capital. Working with US and ARVN troops from the 7th Division, the MRF encountered the 263rd VC battalion and in a series of running battles the allied forces killed over 500 of the guerrillas. However, the 263rd fought hard and eighteen Riverine boats were hit by rockets, grenades, and recoilless rifle fire. Though none were sunk, this was the heaviest fire that the MRF had yet come under. This underlined the ability of the boats to take a great deal of punishment and also the need for additional armament to counter the growing number of heavy caliber weapons being employed by the communists. During CORONADO V the first ASPBs arrived and received their baptism of fire. Toward the end of the operation the first attempt to use flamethrowers took place in Kien Hoa province near Dong Tam with satisfactory results. An M-132 flamethrower armored personnel carrier (APC) was placed in an ATC and tested under high wind conditions. No problems were encountered and additional M-132s were requested until a suitably modified monitor could be substituted for the ATC/APC arrangement.

To help protect Vietnamese civilians during the 1967 National Elections Coronado VII (20-24 October) was conducted. During the elections the MRF dispersed itself throughout the Can Guioc district, but very little contact resulted. Over eighty per cent of the registered voters turned out due to the tight security the riverine craft and personnel provided. The year ended on a more resounding note combat wise, with Coronado IX (1 November to 21 January). This long operation was started, in part, to counter VC attacks against patrolling PBRs in the Giao Pue district.

Working with Vietnamese Marines the MRF met the Viet Cong twice during 1967 in large scale actions. Near the town of Sa Dec in mid-November a VC unit was cornered and in pitched fighting 178 of the enemy were killed. On 4 December at the boundaries between Dinh Tunog and Kien Phong provinces, the allied force ran into both the 267th and 302nd VC battalions. Vietnamese Marines, with the aid of an ATC/APC flamethrower, stormed ashore under withering fire while US units maneuvered to cut off the guerrilla's escape. In two days of fierce fighting over 260 VC were killed against fifty US and Vietnamese casualties. Over forty riverine craft were hit by a variety of communist weapons, but none were sunk, and the majority con-

tinued to take part in the operation. After this battle contact dropped off sharply and the remainder of the operation turned into a mopping up campaign. When CORONADO IX was finally terminated, over 600 *Viet Cong* lay dead. US and Vietnamese fatalities were 100.

Tet

With the success of the various CORONADO OPERATIONS in 1967, *VC* power in the Mekong Delta appeared to be on the wain. However, this appearance was deceiving for in reality the communists were preparing a nation wide offensive operation against US and Vietnamese positions. On 29 January 1968, North Vietnamese and *Viet Cong* forces unleashed their *Tet* offensive, carrying out attacks across the length and breadth of Vietnam. In the Delta region, the *VC* hit the major towns of My Tho, Ben Tie, Cai Lay, Cai Be and Vinh Long on 31 January.

The MRF, in the midst of CORONADO X, redirected its attention toward My Tho where the situation was ciritical. Two battalions of troops were landed in the town and slowly cleared the guerillas out in bitter house to house fighting. Within three days the town was deemed secure enough for the troops to be reembarked and redeployed toward Cai Lay, to cut off retreating enemy troops. Unfortunately most of these guerrillas evaded the MRF and little contact was made. After this fruitless foray, the MRF was dispatched to Vinh Long to support hardpressed ARVN troops. Moving into positions south of the city, the Riverine craft and infantry successfully blocked the *VC*'s line of retreat and bitter fighting resulted as the guerrillas tried to break out of the area. However, the cordon was too tight and by 6 February the communist threat to Vinh Long was broken. These moves by the MRF over the short span of a week proved the ability of the riverine force to react rapidly and move quickly over a large area. During this week the MRF inflicted over 600 enemy casualties in the fighting around My Tho and Vinh Long. Had it not been for TF 117, these important towns might have fallen to the enemy. But, with the ability to quickly move large numbers of troops from one hotspot to another the Riverines were able to effectively counter enemy attacks before they could gain momentum and achieve significant results. Perhaps the role of the MRF during *Tet* can best be summed up by General Westmoreland, the US commander in Vietnam, when he stated that "...the Mobile Riverine Force saved the Delta."

1968 The Second Year

Following the *Tet* offensive, the Mobile Riverine Force continued to expand; in June of 1968 a third River Assault Squadron was formed, and, in July the entire force was reorganized into two sections: Mobile River Group Alpha and Mobile River Group Bravo. Another River Assault Squadron arrived in-country during September, and by fall the MRF had reached its full authorized strength in both combat and support ships. At this time, there were also changes made within the structure of the riverine infantry units which allowed more troops to be used as maneuvering elements, cutting down the number of men kept ashore at Dong Tam.

Along with these organizational changes and increases in force levels, the MRF also expanded its operating areas. Riverine forces with elements of the 2nd Brigade carried out a series of sweeps in Kieu Hoa province under OPERATION HOMESTEAD*. Action was light, as the enemy relied on small ambush teams armed with rocket launchers (RPG-2 or 7) to harass the force. In October the two newly reorganized Mobile River Groups (Alpha and Bravo) of TF 117 carried out additional missions throughout a number of provinces. Mobile Riverine Group Alpha remained in Kieu Hoa while

The use of the code name Coronado for operations was discontinued in the summer of 1968.

A few ATCs were modified to carry a high velocity spray system to wash away ground cover or erode enemy fortifications near the water. Water was sucked up through a pipe which ran over the stern. (US Navy)

To provide support and quarters for the sailors and troops of the MRF, World War Two barracks ships were converted for use in Vietnam. These ships had a helicopter platform added, additional standoff armor, and were air-conditioned. The USS Benewah (APB-35) was also configured as the command control flagship for the flotilla brigade. The second APB, the Colleton, was configured as a squadron and battalion command ship. (US Navy)

Keeping the various boats in service was a never ending task. Maintenance and repair support was provided by a number of landing craft repair ships which moved with the MRF throughout the delta. The Askari (ARL-30) is seen with two Ammi pontoons alongside her hull. Moored to these are a number of ATCs and one standard LCM-6. The cranes near the bow and amidship were capable of lifting an ATC aboard the pontoons for repair and servicing. (US Navy)

These ATCs and Monitors from RAD 91 sit along side an Ammi pontoon prior to an assault into the Delta. Even in the relatively confined waters of the Delta riverways the water could get choppy as is evident from the spray raised by the bows of the moored boats. (US Navy)

Bravo worked in Vinh Binh, Vinh Long, Long An, Dinh Tuong, and Phong Dinh provinces. During October the two groups were reorganized vis-a-vis their River Assault Divisions (RADs). Group Alpha had five Divisions assigned to it while Group Bravo received three.

This shifting of assets resulted in each Group taking responsibility for a specific geographical section of the Mekong Delta in November. Group Alpha, with Riverine Assault Divisions 91, 92, 111, 112, and 151, operated in the eastern delta while Group Bravo, with RADs 121, 132, and 152, worked the western delta. Coinciding with this reorganization came renewed *VC* attacks against MRF support ships. On 1 November *VC* sappers placed mines on the hull of the Westchester County (LST-1167), the resulting explosions on the starboard amidship ruptured the berthing, fuel and storage compartments, killing 26 sailors. After beaching for temporary repairs at Dong Tam the Westchester County went to Yokosuka, Japan for repairs; returning to Vietnam in March of 1969. Two weeks later a salvage barge was sunk by a mine with the loss of two lives. These attacks set the pattern for much of the

Originally Monitors were assigned the job of leading ATCs down the waterways. This Monitor closely watches the river bank for signs of enemy activity as it leads a pair of ATCs down a canal during a patrol operation. These craft are from RAD 92. (US Navy)

The differences between an ATC and Monitor can be seen here. The most evident difference is the spoon bow of the Monitor mounting a 40mm turret. (US Navy)

(Above) As they became available Assault Support Patrol Boats (ASPBs) took over the job of leading columns down the various waterways and because of their ability to sweep mines they proved especially valuable. This ASPB patrols along a canal while troops ashore set up a battery of 105mm howitzers to support troops during OPERATION CORONADO IX. (US Navy)

Fire support was an important part of the riverine force's job during an operation. This Monitor fires its 40mm cannon on enemy positions during operations in the Delta. Note how the crew take advantage of the turret and superstructure for protection while observing the effect of the fire. (US Navy)

Speedy evacuation of casualties could mean the difference between life or death for the wounded. This medivac Huey comes in for a landing atop a specially modified troop carrier. These modified troop carriers were given the designation ATC(H) and often provided full medical assistance for wounded until they could be evacuated to more sophisticated facilities. (US Navy via Cressman)

remaining enemy action encountered by the MRF, and rarely were large groups of guerrillas spotted and brought to combat. Losses during Coronado operations and Tet, plus a healthy respect for the firepower of the Riverine forces, caused the *VC* to revert back to guerrilla warfare where they concentrated on small scale hit and run operations. Throughout the remainder of 1968, TF 117 concentrated on pacifying the delta region and supporting ARVN troops. In addition, as the need arose, forces were assigned to OPERATION SEALORDS in cooperation with Market Time and Game Warden units.

Vietnamization

During 1968 much thought was given to turning over more of the Riverine war effort to the Vietnamese. The first step in this process came about in January of 1969 when the boats of RAD 91 were withdrawn from combat to ready them for turnover to the Vietnamese. This was done on 1 February 1969, and shortly thereafter RAD 91 was officially dissolved. From these assets, along with eight ASPBs, the Vietnamese Navy formed River Assault and Interdiction Divisions (RAIDs) 70 and 71. This set the pattern for the remainder of 1969 as the Riverine force prepared to handover more of its assets to Vietnamese control. Operations continued to be carried out by the Riverine force but as the year progressed more and more effort was concentrated on training Vietnamese personnel to handle and maintain the various boats.

But while the strength of the MRF was being reduced, there was still a war going on, and the soldiers and sailors of the Riverine units continued to carry on with day to day operations. During these missions, the greatest threat to the Riverine boats came from mines and underwater swimmers. A number of boats were sunk by mines and on numerous occasions *VC* sappers tried to attach charges to ships at anchor. Fortunately, these swimmers were kept in check by constant patrols around the anchorages. On occasion the *VC* staged ambushes along the rivers or canals with rocket launchers, recoilless rifles, and automatic weapons. But while casualties were usually light, and damage to the boats minimal, the sailors had to be ever on the alert against these attacks. The guerrillas also made mortar and rocket attacks at night against anchorages but the boat's ability to move about helped to lessen the danger from this type of attack.

At the same time that the Riverine forces were turning over their assets to the Vietnamese, moves were a foot to redeploy the Riverine troops of the 9th Infantry back to the US. This was done gradually, starting in June, and resulted in a steady reduction in infantry assault units available for operations in the Delta. Their place was taken by ARVN units who worked with both their own Riverine forces and the remaining units of the MRF. This reduction in troop strength caused a drop in the tempo of operations and lessened the number of contacts with the *VC*. By the early fall of 1969 withdrawal of the 2nd Brigade was complete allowing the barracks ships, save one, to be withdrawn and returned stateside. Two more River Assault Divisions were turned over to the Vietnamese Navy, and the remaining units of TF 117 began working with a new unit, Task Force 194, which was given the job of conducting SEALORDS.

(Above) M-112-2 shows just how close the riverine craft came to the shore during operations. From River Assault Division 112, this Monitor is taking part in CORONADO V, a combined airmobile, mechanized, and riverine operation against the Cam Son secret zone. (US Navy)

(Below) An H-23 observation helicopter hovers over an ATC(H) during operations along a canal in the Mekong Delta. H-23s were assigned to the MRF during CORONADO V and provided valuable information to task group commanders on possible ambush sites, location of allied forces, and served as relays for communications between the various riverine forces. From CORONADO V onward helicopters served with the MRF as an integral part of the unit's organization. (US Navy via Cressman)

(Above) During an operation riverine boats were often beached to cordon off an area. These VC suspects are being questioned on board a CCB after their capture. From the way the crew is relaxing the fighting is evidently over or not taking place in the immediate vicinity. (US Navy)

(Below) The river war in Vietnam was not all one sided. This ASPB has been run aground by its crew to prevent it from sinking after being hit by a Viet Cong rocket. While some of the crew try to plug the hole the rest return fire on the suspected enemy position. (US Navy)

SEALORDS

By the fall of 1968, the three principal Navy task forces in Vietnam — TF 115 (Market Time), TF 116 (Game Warden), and TF 117 (Mobile Riverine Force) had basically accomplished their respective missions. Along the coast the *Viet Cong* were rarely able to infiltrate men and supplies from the sea while in the Mekong Delta their hard core units and logistic lines had suffered severe losses. Unfortunately, despite this interdiction of supplies, the communists were still a force to be reckoned with in the northern and western parts of the Delta where men and supplies were coming in from Cambodia through the maze of rivers and canals. Men and supplies coming in from the Cambodian sanctuaries was the major reason for the *VC*'s ability to survive the numerous defeats suffered at the hands of the Brown Water Navy.

In 1964 the Bucklew team, which had recommended an increase in US Naval participation in coastal patrol, realized that such an effort was doomed to eventual failure unless a border interdiction plan was instituted to supplement it. However, at that time, and for the next three years, the men and equipment needed to implement such a plan had not been available, but by the fall of 1968, decreasing *VC* activity in the Task Forces' respective areas of responsibility created a surplus of personnel and equipment which could now be employed in border interdiction operations. A plan was developed in October to utilize both the river and coastal assets under the Code name SEALORDS (Southeast Asia Lake, Ocean, River, and Delta Strategy). SEALORDS welded together various units of Game Warden, Market Time, and the Mobile Riverine Force into a combined force who's mission was to interdict the *VC*'s movement of men and supplies through an area that stretched from the Gulf of Thailand to the Parrot's Beak. To implement this plan a new organization, Task Force 194, was created to coordinate the diverse units assigned to the SEALORDS force.

Task Force 194 was given four primary directives by US Headquarters in Saigon.

1. *Interdict VC lines of communications from the Gulf of Thailand to the Bassac River.*
2. *Open the trans-delta waterways and pacify the adjacent areas.*
3. *Clear the Bassac islands and pacify these areas.*
4. *Harass the enemy and keep him off balance.*

Market Time Swift boats began to enlarge their patrol areas by moving further up the rivers and taking over the sectors which the PBRs had been responsible for. In addition these coastal boats began to penetrate the numerous rivers of the Cau Mau Peninsula to stir up the guerrillas in this region. As the Swift boats moved inland and took on additional river responsibilities, Game Warden PBRs pushed deeper inland for deployment at the

proposed barriers which roughly paralleled the Cambodian border. The lack of ground forces within the MRF allowed the heavily armored shallow draft riverine boats, especially the ASPBs, to be used for blocking and interdiction missions along with the PCFs and PBRs.

The first operation carried out by SEALORDS was SEARCH TURN, begun on 2 November. This action was initiated when MRF forces made a series of assaults on enemy positions along the Rach Gia di Long Xuyin Canal. Fighting was relatively light, with only twenty-one guerrillas being killed, though sizeable quantities of weapons, ammunition, and supplies were uncovered. The assault phase of the operation lasted only five days but after the completion of this phase, continued patrols were carried out along the canal from a newly established base on the canal. These patrols paid particular attention to the western end of the barrier and the canals running north from the Rach Gia to Ha Tien which were believed to be part of the main *Viet Cong* supply and communication lines.

Close on the heels of OPERATION SEARCH TURN came FOUL DECK (later renamed OPERATION TRAN HUNG DAO), which started on 16 November. The catalyst which actually started this operation occurred earlier on 14 October when Lieutenant (JG) Michael Bernique, a reserve officer, took his Swift Boat up the Rach Grang Thanh waterway in response to information given him by local residents. The waterway closely paralleled the Cambodian border and was 'off limits' to US forces because of possible political repercussions over a border incident. Acting on his own, Bernique proceeded up the river and surprised a group of guerrillas who scattered, but not before losing three men and leaving behind weapons, documents, and supplies. After regrouping, the *VC* tried to recapture these materials but lost additional men without getting near the captured articles. When word of the fight reached Saigon, Naval headquarters went into an uproar. Bernique, ordered to Saigon, gave a direct account of the action to the admiral in charge of all Navy forces in Vietnam. Fortunately for the young lieutenant, the admiral chose to award him a Silver Star instead of a court martial for going into the 'off limits' area. Word of this decision filtered down to the lower ranks and henceforth the Rach Gran Than became known as 'Bernique's Creek'.

As a result of this incident the admiral took a special interest in the border barrier, and in conjunction with Army authorities, plans were laid to move naval units into the area. The operation began when three Swift boats, led by none other than the intrepid Bernique, again entered the Rach Grang Thanh with orders to proceed up the Vinh Te canal. This group ran into two groups of guerrillas who were put under fire with undetermined results. However, a few hours later South Vietnamese authorities reported that Bernique's group had killed not *VC*, but instead a group of Cambodian bandits, and ten South Vietnamese women. As if to strengthen this report Cambodia also protested and Bernique was once again called on the carpet. Fortunately for him, the resulting investigation showed that all these accusations were false. Eventually it was determined that these charges were part of a skillfully executed com-

When the chance to employ various brown water units of the three major task forces together arose in late 1968, the Navy formed Task Force 194 to coordinate them. Its purpose was to stop the flow of arms and supplies into Vietnam from Cambodia by creating a series of barriers along the border between the two countries. Because of their shallow draft the PBRs moved far up river to cut Viet Cong infiltration routes. This PBR crew scans a canal during the first of these missions, OPERATION SEARCH TURN in November of 1968. (US Navy)

While the PBRs moved upriver the Swift boats took over much of their patrol area and also pushed up the major waterways of the Ca Mau peninsula. The crew of this PCF moves in close to a river bank for a firing run during OPERATION GIANT SLINGSHOT. Note the unusual shield and large ammo box on the stern machinegun mount. The relatively high position of the forward gun turret provided the gunner with excellent visibility as well as a wide field of fire. (US Navy)

munist plot to force the abandonment of the barrier patrols through political pressure. As a result the patrols were continued and pressure was increased on *VC* supply lines. Swift boats kept the western end of the Rach Grang Thanh under surveillance while PBRs and riverine craft did the same on the eastern portion of the river. Despite problems with water levels, high banks, and little ground support, continuous patrols swept the waterways except for a short period in late January and early February of 1969. In the later stages of the operation Vietnamese Naval units took on a greater share of the responsibility and the code name was changed to Tran Hung Dao to signify the increased Vietnamese presence. Eventually FOUL DECK became the second most active of the four interdiction barriers in terms of enemy contacts and captured material.

The third and most active of the four barrier patrols was OPERATION GIANT SLINGSHOT, launched on 6 December. This operation centered on the infamous *Viet Cong* sanctuary known as the 'Parrot's Beak', and was bordered by the Vam Co Tay and Vam Co Dong rivers. These rivers came together at a point approximately fifteen miles south of Saigon to form the Vam Co river which then flowed to the South China Sea. On a map these rivers resembled a slingshot, and, this unusual feature resulted in the choice of the code name for the operation.

Because of low water in the rivers, normal support vessels could not navigate up the waterways. To provide support for the various river craft specially constructed floating facilities were fabricated. Built on a series of 'Ammi' barges, these mobile platforms, called Advance Tactical Support Bases (ATSBs), were sited at Tuyen Nhon and Moc Hoa on the Vam Co Tay River, and Tra Cu and Hiep Hoa on the Vam Co Dong River. Later the ATSB at Hiep Hoa was moved to a more favorable position at Ben Keo near Tay Ninh. Additional support for the Naval units was provided by the Askari (ARL-30) near Tan An and the Harnett County (LST-82) at Ben Luc until the arrival of a specially constructed barge complex at Tan An and the completion of a shore facility at Ben Luc.

During GIANT SLINGSHOT, the Riverine forces working with US troops frequently clashed with the guerrillas who tried to maintain their lines of communication running from the sanctuaries in Cambodia. Over a 1000 firefights occurred during the operation which cost the communists close to 2000 killed. In addition 232 prisoners were taken and over 500 tons of weapons, ammunition, and supplies were seized. These losses proved beyond a doubt that the 'Parrot's Beak' was a major supply route from communist sanctuaries in Cambodia. And the violent reaction by the guerrillas also showed how important they felt these routes were. The number of contacts with allied forces during GIANT SLINGSHOT was more than double all the other operations combined. However, despite a fierce effort the *VC* was unable to thwart the drive by US and Vietnamese forces, nor could they keep open their infiltration routes. This forced the *VC* to shift their logistics effort further west to a gap between the GIANT SLINGSHOT area and the FOUL DECK barrier.

To counter this *VC* shift, the final interdiction operation, BARRIER REEF was launched on 2 January 1969. This barrier ran from the one established during GIANT SLINGSHOT to the two parallel ones established during FOUL DECK and SEARCH TURN. BARRIER REEF completed the interdiction line across the northern reaches of the Mekong Delta, allowing allied forces to carry out continuous patrols from the Gulf of Thailand to the 'Parrot's Beak'. As a result the flow of men and material to communist forces in the Delta region dropped to a trickle, which allowed South Vietnamese forces to increase their pacification efforts and make great strides in bringing this area of the Delta under effective government control. It also allowed allied units to concentrate a large force on short notice to counter any detected enemy buildup without disrupting existing organizational and logistical structures.

An unusual innovation tried during the spring of 1969 was the movement

A monitor from RAD 112 passes a small hamlet located on one of the small canals which was used by the guerrillas to move men and supplies from Cambodia to the southern part of the Delta. These patrols did much to cut down on the flow of troops and material from the communist sanctuaries in Cambodia. (US Navy)

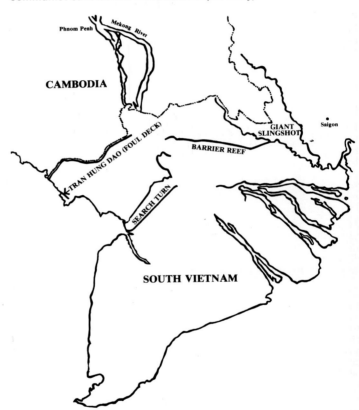

Elements of the Mobile Riverine Force joined with the PBRs and PCFs to attack the communist supply lines. This ASPB leads an ATC up a river during a sweep of the Vam Co Dong river during GIANT SLINGSHOT. GIANT SLINGSHOT was the most successful of the four operations carried out by brown water naval forces engaged in SEALORDS activities. (US Navy)

During the late spring of 1969 a new tactic was tried when PBRs were lifted by giant CH-54 Flying Cranes to areas where they had never operated before. This caught the VC totally by surprise and resulted in heavy enemy losses. (US Navy)

During this period more and more American brown water assets were turned over to the Vietnamese. Among these were Mark II Swift boats seen just after their turnover. One of the main distinguishing features between the Mark I and II was the railing toward the bow and the porthole shapes along the superstructure. (O'Mara)

of PBRs into supposedly inaccessible waterways using Army CH-54 Flying Cranes. This was done in May when six PBRs were lifted into the upper Saigon River and again in June when another six were set down in the Cai Cai canal. Both operations caught the communists by surprise; it was through such moves as this that the allies kept the *VC* constantly off balance as to where they might be struck next.

By 1970, the growing pressure of Vietnamization began to be felt in the SEALORDS forces, and as more and more Riverine craft were turned over to the Vietnamese, they began to take on a bigger share of the barrier patrols. By 1971 the Vietnamese had assumed almost all responsibilities for these operations as the US Naval forces in Vietnam were cut back. The only US Naval personnel still working on the interdiction program were advisors with the various Vietnamese units involved in the patrols. This US strength was further cut back in the early spring and summer of 1972 until only a few American officers were left in a liaison capacity within the Vietnamese command structure. These Vietnamese units did a creditable job though their maintenance facilities were never able to keep the various river forces up to strength.

While the military situation deteriorated after the American withdrawal, the Delta area remained basically secure due to the efforts of the Vietnamese Navy. After the fall of South Vietnam in the spring of 1975, dissident Army and Navy units continued to oppose the NVA Army using guerrilla tactics which they had learned so well from the *Viet Cong*. To this day, these elements still constitute a force which the communists have not been able to fully eliminate.

(Above) PCFs often teamed up with Vietnamese units in sweeps through the Mekong Delta. These Swift boats have just dropped off Popular Forces (PFs) in a village to check for Viet Cong activity. Although the boats were not designed for this type of use they were able to carry a fairly large number of troops in the restricted waterways of the delta. (O'Mara)

Often times Popular Forces were ferried to their destination by an array of vessels. PCFs cover a landing by Vietnamese troops during a SEALORDS operation. The PFs were not very popular with US Navy crews because they often stole equipment and personel belongings of the crews. (O'Mara)

The End

As the United States pursued the policy of 'Vietnamization' more and more of the war effort was turned over to the South Vietnamese Armed Forces. In early 1969 River Assault Division 91 was deactivated, and from its assets the Vietnamese formed River Assault and Interdiction Division (RAID) 70 and 71. These two Vietnamese brown water units took part in OPERATION GIANT SLINGSHOT, helping US forces cut communist supply lines coming out of the 'Parrot's Beak'. Vietnamese units also participated heavily in the later stages of FOUL DECK and in recognition of their active involvement, the operation was renamed TRAN HUNG DAO.

By this time plans were in progress to turn over to the South Vietnamese Navy all the 82 foot WPBs then being operated by the US Coast Guard in Market Time. By May enough Vietnamese had been trained so that two cutters, the Point Garnett and Point League, could be transferred to their control. In appropriate ceremonies at Saigon, the two ships were renamed the Le Phuoc Duc and Le Van Nga. Turnover of the 82 footers continued throughout 1969 and 1970. By August of 1970 the transfers were complete when the last two cutters, the Point Marone and Point Cypress, were taken over by the Vietnamese Navy.

During 1970 US brown water withdrawal rate increased dramatically. By the early part of the year there were very few wholly American crewed combat craft. Under the ACTOV program the Vietnamese took over control of nearly 250 boats by late spring. In conjunction with these transfers, US naval manpower in-country was cut by twenty-five per cent. Close on the heels of these turn overs came the invasion of the communist sanctuaries in Cambodia. US and Vietnamese river units supported American and ARVN ground forces as they moved against these longtime enemy sanctuaries. Responding to the convulsive outcry from the anti-war movement over the invasion of a 'neutral Country', President Nixon imposed a limit as to how far US forces could advance into the Cambodia. Due to this restriction Vietnamese Naval units were tasked with opening the Mekong River to the capital of Phnom Penh. Covered by US airpower, including HAL-3 helicopters and VAL-4 Broncos, Vietnamese boats managed to clear the waterway to the Cambodian capitol. Once these clearing operations were completed Vietnamese Naval units periodically swept the river and escorted convoys through *Viet Cong* and *Khmer Rouge* ambush sites.

Following the Cambodian invasion the American withdrawal moved into high gear. By mid-summer over eighty per cent of all operational brown water craft had been transferred to the Vietnamese. Coupled with this, an additional twenty-five per cent of the remaining US Navy manpower was redeployed to the United States or other US Navy duty stations, almost totally eliminating American Naval participation in combat operations. Most of the US Naval personnel still in Vietnam were primarily concentrated in support, advisory, or liaison roles except for select units such as the SEALS and aviation squadrons.

By 1969 Vietnamization of the war began to get under way. For the various coastal and river forces this meant a gradual turnover of assets to the Vietnamese Navy. These Swift boats were turned over in 1969 and became part of Squadron Two of the Vietnamese coastal patrol force. (US Army)

PBR units assumed the job of training Vietnamese sailors on a one to one indoctrination program. By the late summer of 1969 there were almost no PBRs in Vietnam manned by solely US personnel. These Vietnamese PBRs are moored alongside YRBM 16, a repair and support barge manned by US sailors. Even after the turnover of operational units to the Vietnamese, logistical support was still provided by American personnel. (US Navy)

Gradually, during 1971 and 1972, the remaining support functions being performed by US Naval personnel were turned over to the Vietnamese. By the spring of 1972 approximately 2000 US sailors were still in-country. With the signing of the peace accord in January of 1973, the US pulled out its remaining men in Vietnam. From this point on the Vietnamese were on their own. For the Vietnamese Navy, the period immediately following the ceasefire was relatively calm in the Delta region in comparison to the other areas of South Vietnam where large numbers of *Viet Cong* and North Vietnamese regulars were dug in. The biggest problem which the Vietnamese Navy faced were maintenance and the procurement of spare parts. Unlike

The Vietnamese received a number of 100 foot Patrol Motor Gunboats (PG) such as the one seen here. They were armed with a 40mm cannon, four 20mm cannon, and two .50 caliber machine guns. These boats proved very efficient for coastal patrol and for close inshore work due to their shallow draft. (US Navy via Cressman)

During the invasion of Cambodia in the spring of 1970 Vietnamese brown water Naval units joined with US brown water forces to push up the rivers in pursuit of communist forces. This Vietnamese PBR moves up the Mekong River toward Phnom Penh after restrictions were placed on how far US forces were allowed to advance into Cambodia. (US Army)

An unusual modification to a Vietnamese ASPB. The forward gun position has had two sets of rocket launchers mounted co-axially with the 20mm gun. The author saw a number of these mounts during visits to Vietnamese Naval bases in 1971 and 1972. This particular photo was taken at Nha Be in late 1971. (Mesko)

American sailors who had usually spent their lives around machinery, the Vietnamese had no mechanical background and were not strong on preventive maintenance. To them if an airplane, boat or tank ran, it should be left alone. Unfortunately, this attitude soon reduced the number of operational craft and flooded the repair facilities with a huge backlog of work. Aggravating this situation was the lack of adequate spare parts. For a short period of time immediately after the US withdrawal, adequate supplies of replacement parts were fairly easy to come by. However, as American aid dwindled, so did the availability of spare parts and even those on hand became difficult to obtain by the repair facilities since the Vietnamese had no

A Vietnamese monitor from RAD 70 sits quietly along side the shoreline of the Cai Lon canal during a lull in operations. Unfortunately, once the Vietnamese took over the various river and coastal vessels they failed to properly maintain them and as a result the number of operational units fell far below what was normal when Americans had manned these craft. (US Navy)

central facility for disbursement and spare parts were scattered all over Vietnam. This seriously weakened overall Naval strength and large numbers of boats were usually out of commission due to minor difficulties.

After the peace accord was signed, fighting continued on a reduced level as both sides attempted to strengthen their respective positions. The South Vietnamese brown water force tried to keep the Mekong River open to Phnom Penh and insure a steady flow of fuel, ammunition and rice to the the beleaguered Cambodian regime of Lon Nol. Heavy fighting occurred around the river town of Hong Ngu, the site of an important Vietnamese Naval base. The NVA made repeated attempts to block the river to supply convoys and reopen their own infiltration routes. With the help of the Vietnamese Air Force and supported by brown water craft ARVN troops were able to clear the area of communist troops and keep the river open to the Cambodian capitol.

Throughout the rest of the Delta, the Vietnamese Navy did a creditable job, albeit, within the limits of its operational strength due to serviceability. In particular, the Vietnamese brown water navy was very effective against infiltration routes along the Cai Lon River in Kien Grang and Chuong Thien provinces. With nearly 400 river craft, the Vietnamese were able to keep up the pressure on the NVA and VC despite their poor maintenance performance. Unfortunately, neither the Army nor the Navy really worked closely with one another in the Delta and this lack of cooperation seriously hampered operations. Higher authority did little to remedy the situation and the two forces never learned to coordinate their respective actions.

In 1974 things took a turn for the worse. Due to Congressional cuts in US aid, the Vietnam Navy was forced to deactivate twenty-one of its forty-four riverine units. As a result of these cuts, the brown water navy was unable to effectively patrol the Delta and could no longer provide security along several of the major canals. The VC began exerting increasing pressure throughout the region. Convoys going up the Mekong river to Phnom Penh came under heavier and heavier fire. Due to their diminishing forces the Vietnamese were forced to curtail their support of this vital lifeline to Phnom Penh. The last attempt to push a convoy through to the Cambodian capitol occurred in late January of 1975 when a small group of tugs, barges and ships managed to reach the city with enough supplies to last the population two weeks. After the losses suffered by this nearly unprotected supply run, authorities decided to resupply the capital exclusively by air.

Throughout Vietnam, the communists began a series of attacks in early 1975 designed to slowly whittle away at the government's strength. The brunt of these actions took place in Military Regions I, II, and III where the NVA launched a series of ground assaults spearheaded by armor and backed by massive artillery barrages. In the Mekong Delta region no large scale attacks took place; instead the communists carried out small hit and runs designed to pin down government forces so they could not be shifted to the more critical areas. As a result the three divisions south of Saigon played no direct role in the debacle which occurred further north. The few ocean going ships could do little except evacuate troops from besieged coastal cities. By the end of April it was all over. The NVA swept aside ARVN resistance in the three military regions. A prolonged defense of the Mekong Delta probably would have been possible, but it would have served no useful purpose. With this in mind the South Vietnamese government unconditionally surrendered to the North Vietnamese on 30 April 1975.

Since the fall of South Vietnam, there have been continuous reports of guerrilla resistance which has developed to oppose the new communist regime. Centered in the Mekong Delta, the reports indicate that the movement is composed of ex-Vietnamese Marines, SEALs, sailors, and ARVN troops. To combat this enemy, these reports state that the communists have had to use former US and Vietnamese riverine craft. If this is true it is indeed ironic that the roles have been reversed and the communists are now being forced to fight the same kind of war which they themselves waged for so long.

This ASPB has had the original single machine gun mount replaced by a twin mount. Note how the guns can receive ammunition from both sides. Unfortunately while the twin .50 caliber machinegun mount gave the Vietnamese a tremendous amount of firepower its range often led to civilian casualties outside the immediate battle area which did little to endear the Vietnamese Navy to local inhabitants. (Mesko)

The last significant operation by the Vietnamese navy was when it helped convoys move up the Mekong River to resupply the Cambodian capital of Phnom Penh. Vietnamese LSSLs, PCFs and a LSM dock at the Cambodian capital after a successful supply run. However pressing problems in their own country forced the Vietnamese to cease these missions and the Khmer Rouge were eventually able to close the river to such convoys. (US Army)

Another interesting modification was the replacing of the 40mm turret on this Monitor with the turret from an LVTH-6 Amtrac mounting a 105mm howitzer. Bar armor protection has been added around the turret. (Mesko)